THE TRAMWAYS
OF READING.

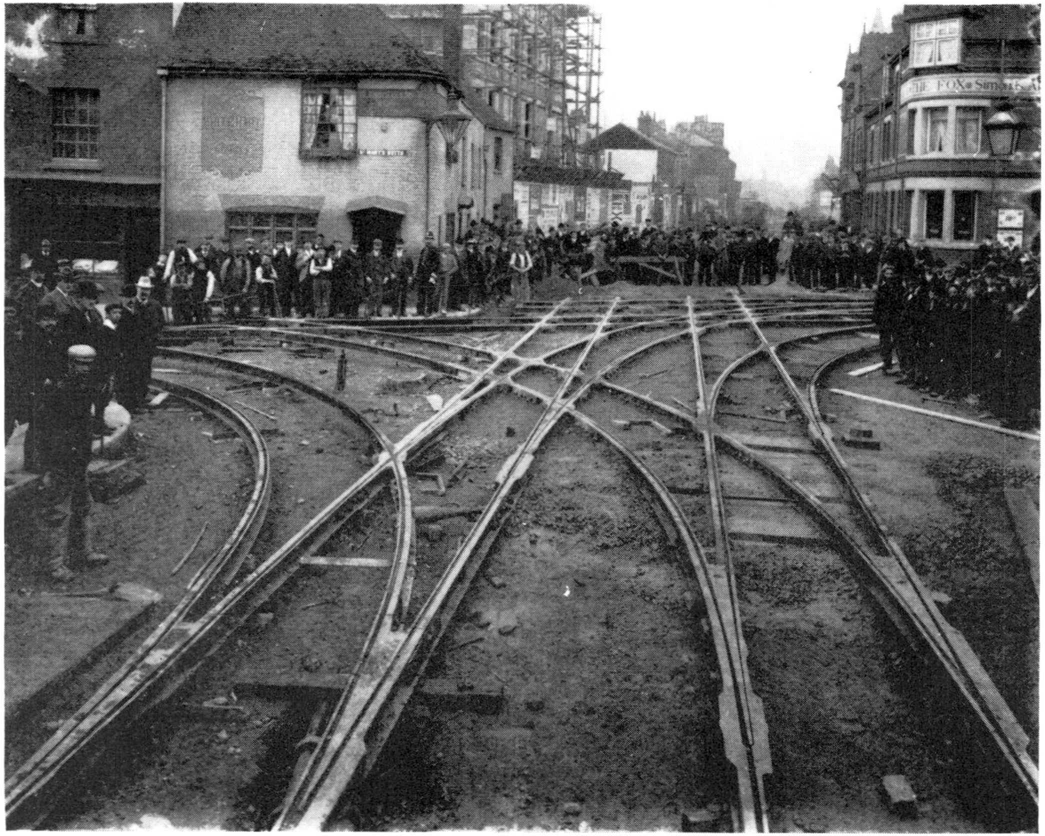

Photo Courtesy Walton Adams & Son, Ltd.

THE TRAMWAYS
OF READING

BY

H. E. JORDAN.

To the Memory of Lilian

PUBLISHED BY

ADAM GORDON, PRIORY COTTAGE,

CHETWODE, BUCKS, MK18 4LB

PRINTED BY
THE IPSWICH BOOK COMPANY

AUTHOR'S NOTES.

From the day I was born I can claim a close connection with the Reading tramways. My father spent forty years of his working life in the service of the undertaking, being successively conductor, motorman, trolleybus driver and inspector, so it was fairly natural that I should develop an interest in the trams at an early age. I was soon introduced to the intricacies of duty schedules and timetables by reason of the fact that I frequently had to meet " Dad's tram " with a can of hot tea or cocoa and sandwiches. Absolutely accurate timekeeping was essential for if the connection was missed there was nearly an hour before he again passed the spot. On occasion my mother would get a little behind schedule with the preparation of the meal and this called for a hectic dash down the street with the cans, great care having to be exercised to avoid spilling any of the beverage. I could swing a can full of tea over my head in professional style (but not when my mother was looking).

An old and faded photograph in my possession shows the Reading Tramways football team grouped with the General Manager, Mr. J. M. Calder, on whose knees sits the diminutive figure of the team mascot, rigged out in a miniature version of the team's colours (which were the same as the tram's livery). The mascot is none other than the present writer.

I soon learned to identify an approaching car and its driver long before they reached me, the former by its advertisements or perhaps the distinctive sound of its motors or note of the gong, the latter by his stance at the controls or the angle at which he wore his cap. One feature of a tramwayman's life, particularly on a relatively small system such as Reading, was the way in which car crews became " public figures." The motormen on their open platforms became known by sight to hundreds, probably thousands of people who saw them daily. No present-day bus driver shut up in his little cabin can ever be on such familiar terms with his passengers. It was always a puzzle to me as a young child, that when out with my father almost every other person we passed would acknowledge him with a " Hello Tim," but he could not tell me the names of half of them. Where the nickname " Tim " was derived from I never knew, but that was the name by which everyone knew him, and I am still called " Young Tim " by old tram men, although the adjective is becoming open to question nowadays.

My association with the Reading trams was therefore close and personal, an association which has at last, after many years, prompted me to write this history. My father, like the trams he drove, has now passed from us and it is to his memory that I would like to dedicate this book, the preparation of which has afforded me many hours of pleasant research through old Committee minutes, local papers, books and maps, for access to which I am immeasurably indebted to the staff of the Reading Public Library Reference Department. They never failed to produce anything I asked for, and must have heaved a great sigh of relief when I at last completed the work.

5

My thanks are also due to the English Electric Co., Ltd., and the Metropolitan-Vickers Electrical Co., Ltd., for supplying certain technical details and to Mr. George Davies for assisting with several matters when my memory was a little hazy. For some of the information concerning fare tickets I am indebted to Mr. W. H. Bett—Mr. R. A. Hobbs also assisting in this direction. Extracts from the ' Reading Standard ' are by kind permission of the Editor of that paper.

Photographs have been credited wherever the source is known, but I must respectfully tender my apologies to anyone concerned in the one or two cases where the origin of an illustration cannot be traced.

I must also thank Mr. G. F. Craven, O.B.E., for writing the Foreword, and Mr. J. C. Gillham for drawing the map. Finally my thanks are due to the Light Railway Transport League for accepting my manuscript for publication and to Mr. J. W. Fowler for his assistance in getting the story into print.

H. E. JORDAN.
December, 1956.

AUTHOR'S NOTES TO SECOND EDITION

Over 30 years have elapsed since the first edition of this work appeared and it has long been out of print. A number of suggestions have been received that it should be re-printed and I am now indebted to Mr. Adam Gordon for undertaking this venture.

No attempt has been made to alter or update the original manuscript, and it should be realised that many references in the present tense in Chapter VIII, to events subsequent to the tramway abandonment should now, in fact, be in the past tense. The trolleybuses which replaced the trams were themselves abandoned on 3rd November 1968.

Inevitably, a certain amount of additional material has come to light in the years since the original publication, and this has been embodied in the present work in the form of Appendices.

Happily, very few errors have been identified in the first edition, but one which must be mentioned is the reference in Chapter III to cars supplied to Birkenhead Corporation by Dick Kerr & Co. I am indebted to Mr. J. H. Price for pointing out that this firm did not supply any cars to Birkenhead. In fact the car used in the artist's drawing referred to, was a product of G. F. Milnes & Co., from the batch numbered 14-44 in the Birkenhead fleet.

My thanks again to Mr. Gordon and to the printers, Ipswich Book Company, for making this second edition possible, and to Mr. J. C. Gillham for the use of his map on page 24.

READING   H. E. JORDAN
June 1990.

CONTENTS.

LIST OF ILLUSTRATIONS.

FOREWORD.

BY

G. F. CRAVEN, O.B.E., A.M.I.C.E., M.I.Mech.E., M.I.E.E.

(General Manager and Engineer—Reading Corporation Tramways,
1912-1919.)

IT is curious that with many of our institutions a really lively interest in them develops only when they get to the stage of disappearing. This has certainly been the case with the tramcar in this country. For some reason, while the Railways have always had a large and enthusiastic following, a similar interest in tramcars seems to have become widely recognised only since the last World War, and enthusiasts who become interested are necessarily dependent upon such works as this for any detailed knowledge of systems which have now been out of existence for, in some instances, 20 years or more.

I am very grateful to Mr. Jordan for giving me the opportunity of writing the Foreword for this very admirable history of the trams in Reading. I was myself very closely associated with the trams there for 15 years and, as Mr. Jordan has recorded, for the last seven of those years, I was General Manager and Engineer.

I was very happy that I was succeeded by Jimmy Calder, to whom the author very rightly pays a warm tribute which I would very readily like to endorse. Mr. Calder and I were very close friends throughout the whole of my service in Reading and right up to the time of his death.

Although when I left Reading in 1920 it was 13 years before I was appointed as General Manager at Halifax, I was, during that time, intimately in touch with tramway development, because I was a tramway expert for one of the largest electrical manufacturers in the country, and I watched with considerable interest the developments carried out by go-ahead undertakings such as the London County Council, whose foresight in adopting up-to-date equipment on their tramways in the middle of the 1920's enabled them to carry out extensive savings in operation. I am sure that had their foresight, and a similar foresight at such places as Glasgow, Leeds and Sheffield, been more widespread, the tram would have come to a much less inglorious end in many of the towns and cities which it served so valiantly for so many years.

It was during my seven years of office that the foundations were laid for Reading's present motor and trolleybus system, and I am proud that before I relinquished my post as General Manger I was able to inaugurate the motor bus in 1919. Twenty years afterwards, I revisited Reading to be present when the last tram was run on the 20th May, 1939. This was the end of an era for Reading's transport, and I am sure that enthusiasts of to-day and historians of tomorrow will have reason to be grateful to Mr. Jordan for the painstaking work which has obviously gone into the compiling of this book.

November, 1956.

CHAPTER I.

THE HORSE TRAMWAYS UNDER COMPANY OPERATION.

The town of Reading, the Official Guide Book tells us, began as a small Saxon settlement on the banks of the River Kennet, its first historical mention being in the year 871 A.D. It was not until the eighteenth century that any real development took place however, when the opening of the Kennet and Avon Canal in 1723 linking London with Bristol brought considerable business to the town which by then covered the area of the triangle bounded by Friar Street in the north, Duke Street and Silver Street in the east and Southampton Street and St. Mary's Butts on the western side.

Houses gradually spread westward along Oxford Road and eastward along King's Road so that the construction of the Great Western Railway in 1840 followed by the arrival of the South Eastern Railway nine years later formed more or less natural boundaries to the north and east. The population of the town had grown to about 21,000, creating the need for local transport which was provided at first by several enterprising inn keepers. One of these, the landlord of the " Peacock " in Broad Street, ran several horse bus services including one to Caversham (" Prince of Wales "), another to the Cemetery Junction and a third to the " Queen's Head " in Christchurch Road, Whitley. Horses from this gentleman's stable were also supplied to the Reading Fire Brigade and Ambulance. Another horse bus service ran to the village of Sonning, several miles east of the town.

It was along the main east to west route that the first moves were made to provide better transport and to this end The Reading Tramways Company was formed in 1878 to construct and operate about 2½ miles of horse tramway authorised by the Reading Tramways Order of that year, details of which were as follows.

TRAMWAY No. 1. A tramway 1 mile 1 furlong 5.6 chains in length commencing in Oxford Road at a point opposite or nearly opposite to the eastern side of Grove Lands Road,* passing thence in an easterly direction along Oxford Road, Oxford Street† and Broad Street and terminating in Broad Street opposite the eastern side of St. Mary's Butts.

TRAMWAY No. 1A. A tramway or passing place 3 chains in length wholly situated in Oxford Road commencing and terminating by junctions with tramway No. 1 at points respectively 23 yards and 89 yards or thereabouts eastward of Grove Lands Road.

TRAMWAY No. 1B. A tramway or passing place 4 chains in length wholly situated in Oxford Road commencing and terminating by junctions with

---

* The Grove Lands Road referred to here is now known as Wilson Road and should not be confused with the present-day Grovelands Road which was then Grovelands Road West. See The Reading Corporation Act, 1900.

† Oxford Street is now an integral part of Oxford Road.

tramway No. 1 at points respectively opposite to and 88 yards or thereabouts eastward of Lorne Street.

Tramway No. 1C. A tramway or passing place 2 chains in length commencing in Oxford Street by a junction with tramway No. 1 at a point 17 yards or thereabouts westward from West Street passing thence along Oxford Street into Broad Street and terminating in Broad Street at a point opposite to the eastern side of St. Mary's Butts.

Tramway No. 2. A tramway 1 mile 1 furlong 2.57 chains in length commencing in Broad Street by a junction with tramway No. 1 at its point of termination hereinbefore described passing thence along Broad Street into and along King Street, King's Road and the roadways of the bridges over the River Kennet and the Kennet Canal and the open space at the junction of King's Road and London Road and terminating in such open space at a point 87 yards or thereabouts westward of the entrance lodge to the Cemetery.

Tramway No. 2A. A tramway 2 furlongs 3.9 chains in length commencing in Broad Street by a junction with tramway No. 1C at its point of termination and passing thence along Broad Street, King Street and King's Road and terminating in King's Road by a junction with tramway No. 2 at a point 40 yards or thereabouts eastward from High Street.

Tramway No. 2B. A tramway 1 furlong 4.18 chains in length commencing in King's Road by a junction with tramway No. 2 at a point situated 34 yards or thereabouts eastward from Watlington Street, passing along King's Road and the roadway of the bridge over the Kennet Canal and terminating in King's Road by a junction with tramway No. 2 at a point opposite the eastern side of Eldon Road.

Tramway No. 2C. A tramway 2 chains in length commencing in King's Road by a junction with tramway No. 2 at a point 131 yards or thereabouts westward from the entrance lodge of the Cemetery passing thence along King's Road into and along the open space at the junction of King's Road and London Road and terminating in such open space at a point 87 yards or thereabouts westward from the entrance lodge to the Cemetery.

It will be noted that tramways Nos. 1A, 1B, 1C, 2A, 2B and 2C refer to the second track in the lengths of double line, and in this connection it should be recorded that two additional passing places were provided later, one just east of the River Kennet bridge (later known as Crown Bridge) in King's Road and the second at Fatherson Road about 300 yards west of the Cemetery terminus. The eastern half of the tramway was thus well provided with passing places, in sharp contrast to the western section, which possessed only one loop between Broad Street and the Barracks terminus.

The Order contained the usual clauses relating to fares and workmen's services, and Section 21 required that "traffic on the tramway shall be suspended between the hours of 11 a.m. and 1.0 p.m. on every Sunday, Good Friday and Christmas Day." This section was repealed, however, by Section 32 of the Reading Tramways Order of 1899.

The exact date on which construction commenced cannot be ascertained but there is a newspaper reference to "lines now being laid" on 18th January, 1879. The Board of Trade Inspector Major-General Hutchinson visited the undertaking on 4th April, 1879 and accompanied by the Mayor, H. B. Blandy, Esq., the Deputy Mayor, the Town Clerk, the Borough Surveyor, and the Tramway Company's engineer, Mr. Kincaid, walked from the Oxford Road terminus to Broad Street to carry out the inspection. The eastern half of the line from Broad Street to Cemetery Junction was presumably not ready for inspection as the party is reported to have returned to the Barracks in a tramcar. Permission was given for the Company to commence operation on the section inspected provided they undertook to carry out certain " repairs." Just what these repairs were (to a brand new line) was not stated in Press reports of the time, but public services began the next day, Saturday, 5th April, 1879, between The Barracks and Broad Street (Bull Hotel). As would be expected with such a novel attraction, business was brisk and it was stated that " rich and poor from far and near came and rubbed shoulders to take a ride on the trams," and over £100 was taken in fares in the first two days.

As the novelty wore off, however, complaints began to be heard, ' The Reading Observer ' of 10th May, 1879, containing a long editorial bemoaning the irregularity of the service, overcrowding, passengers smoking on cars and suggesting that the cars were too heavy for the one horse provided. Trouble was also being experienced with the working of the points, as it was not uncommon to see two cars face to face on the same line at passing loops. It should be remembered that in the early days of horse tramways it was the practice to use open points through which the cars were " steered " by pulling the horses to right or left as required in the hope that the car wheels would take the desired direction. Evidently the drivers had not yet become proficient in this part of their duties.

On the 29th May, 1879, Major-General Hutchinson revisited the town to complete the inspection of the eastern half of the system, with which

Single deck horse car No. 6 at Cemetery Junction terminus in the '80's.

13

he expressed his satisfaction. He was not satisfied, however, with the repairs alleged to have been carried out on the Oxford Road line, remarking that if the company had done their best, it was a very poor best. He could not, therefore, recommend the Board of Trade to authorise the opening of the eastern half, except on conditions that would ensure the repairs to the first portion being satisfactorily completed. This assurance was presumably given as public services over the entire line commenced on 31st May, 1879, with a fleet of six single-decked cars each seating 24, of which four cars were probably required to work the 20 minute service provided at the outset.

An amusing account of a ride on the trams appeared in the local Press at this time, a correspondent to the 'Reading Observer' writing ".... having secured a car and a seat—both difficult operations—our attention becomes fixed by the sudden apparition in the doorway of a mild-looking gentleman in blue serge and auburn whiskers. Furtively looking around upon the passengers, he plunges rather suddenly into a seat not with any intention of remaining in it, however, for almost immediately rising, he takes a seat in the opposite corner. There is something on his mind and he cannot rest. Rising once again he confers with the youthful conductor and offers him in a very deferential manner a quantity of sound advice, but no money. A car passes us and this volatile gentleman springs hurriedly from the footboard and we have the gratification of seeing him at considerable speed, chase the retreating vehicle to afford its occupants the same pleasant surprise that he has given us. I have come to the conclusion that he must be an Inspector, and if so he must get through a large amount of inspecting in the course of the day. His sudden appearances and disappearances never disconcert the conductors who esteem his visits an amusing episode in a rather tedious journey."

Of another fellow passenger, the same correspondent says "... a citizen felt hurt that his faithful dog was not only denied a seat but even the privilege of being chained behind the car. It was explained to him that apart from several minor inconveniences there were two main objections to this course, (a) The dog would stand a reasonable chance of being hanged by the sudden start of the car and (b) if he survived, each of the 23 other occupants of the car might justly claim to have such dogs as they possessed chained on behind and thus the unpleasant and noisy accompaniment of a pack of hounds of all sorts and sizes would be added to the perils of the ride."

To meet increasing demands of the public, on 7th October, 1879, a seventh car was added to the fleet, another single decked vehicle but differing considerably from the earlier cars. Manufactured by the patentee, a Mr. Hughes of Loughborough, the body was arranged to revolve on the truck, saving the labour of detaching the horse at each terminus and re-attaching it to the other end. The body was divided into two compartments, the front section comfortably furnished with cushions for ladies and non-smokers and that at the rear for those wishing to smoke, this latter section being without windows! Accommodation was provided for 28 passengers and it was stated that there were only five other such cars in existence at the time, two in Manchester, two in Glasgow and one at Gloucester.

The mention earlier of youthful conductors may be coupled with innumerable complaints appearing in the Press at this time of inattention to duty, rudeness and inefficiency of these employees, whose chief delight appeared to be to leave would-be passengers standing at the roadside. In

14

reply to the complaints, the manager of the Tramways Company inserted the following notice in the 'Reading Observer' of 14th October, 1879 :—

"I shall be obliged if anyone having a complaint will notify it to me when they will find it will be attended to, but no notice will be taken if it be of an anonymous character."

The writing of anonymous letters and the use of *noms de plume* was prevalent at the time, and a long and heated correspondence was conducted in the Press between "Scotia" and "Progression." The former gentleman was evidently a strict Sabbatarian who could see nothing but sin in the running of Sunday tram services, while the latter took the opposite view.

The fleet of seven cars was worked by a stud of 31 horses, and the original 20 minute frequency was increased to a car every ten minutes, a weekly total of about 14,000 passengers being carried. Further cars were added to stock from time to time, to a total of 13 vehicles but complete details cannot be traced. Nos. 1 to 7 have been shown to be single-decked cars, but a very old photograph of No. 8 exists depicting a double-decked car with knifeboard seating on the top deck. Another picture shows a double-decked car believed to be No. 10, with reversed stairs, although

Photo—R. B. Parr collection.

Double deck horse car with knifeboard seating on upper deck, in Broad Street.

15

direct stairs were in general use. The entire fleet appears to have been replaced in the '90's as all subsequent photographs are of a standard type of car with transverse seating on the top decks.

A universal fare of 2d. any distance was originally charged but from about June, 1882, 1d. stages were introduced at Trinity Church and Factory Bridge. Complete details of the ticket system are not known, but one or two examples exist which are not without interest. One specimen of a 2d. ticket bears sections " Early to Barracks " and " Barracks to Early," the misspelling of Earley being curious enough, added to which the mere use of the name is wishful thinking to say the least, the district of Earley being all of a mile further along Wokingham Road from the Cemetery Junction terminus. This ticket is coloured buff and bears a bold red overprint " Governess " (probably meaning school teacher) while similar examples are known, coloured lemon, with blue overprints " Postman " and " School " respectively. The Company indulged in another bout of wishful thinking during the '90's when, following the opening to the public of Palmer Park in 1891, the legend " Barracks, Cemetery, Palmer Park " was painted on the sides of the cars, although again, the last-named point was well beyond their terminus and horse cars never reached the Park in Company days.

There appears to have been some attempt to extend the tramways in the '80's by a line running north and south from Caversham Bridge to Whitley, but the project was overthrown by certain influential residents of Caversham. Competition in the form of horse buses began to make itself apparent, several operators coming into the field, so the Tramways Company itself began to run horse buses. The competition unfortunately led to a certain amount of reckless driving and overloading and numerous cases came before the magistrates. The Tramways Company was summoned for permitting a car to be overloaded, thirty-nine passengers being counted on a car licensed to carry thirty-three. On 12th September, 1896, a " Favourite " bus was in collision with a tramcar in King's Road, while on the 9th October following, a Tramway omnibus (No. 8) knocked down a lamp post in Oxford Road while overtaking a tramcar. The Corporation began to take notice of this unsatisfactory state of affairs and the Borough Surveyor was requested to report upon the tramways. When completed the report was couched in " terms of sweeping condemnation " and a copy was sent to the Tramways Company with a request for their observations. The Company's reply was a request to the Corporation for permission to apply for a Provisional Order for certain alterations and extensions to the tramways and for powers to work them electrically. These extensions were to include a line into Caversham, terminating at the junction of Prospect Street and Church Street. The Company offered to defray all expenses for a deputation of the Council to visit the recently opened electric tramways at Bristol, both the Reading and Bristol Companies being at the time associated with the parent Imperial Tramways Company. The offer was not accepted, and the Council refused to consent to the proposed Order as it might prejudicially affect their own powers to purchase the tramway about which they were beginning to give serious thought. After much discussion, the Corporation finally decided to apply for a Provisional Order of their own to authorise construction of certain tramways being extensions of the existing Company system. The Order was granted on the 16th August, 1899.

The decision to purchase the Company under Section 43 of the Tramways Act, 1870, was made at the Council meeting on 21st September,

1899, and following Board of Trade approval formal notice of intention to purchase was served upon the Company on the 1st December that year. The Company immediately claimed that the Corporation had no legal rights to purchase having, it was alleged, allowed their powers to lapse, and they further declined to grant facilities for inspection and valuation of the system. The Company furthermore, in April, 1900, applied for an injunction to restrain the Corporation from proceeding with the purchase. Hearing was on 26th July, 1900, before Mr. Justice Buckley in the Queen's Bench Division of the High Court, the case being dismissed with costs, the Company giving notice of appeal. At the time, a similar case was pending in the House of Lords, between Wallasey United Tramways Company and Wallasey Urban District Council, and when on 13th December, 1900, this case was dismissed, the Reading Company withdrew their appeal.

The way was now clear for the Corporation to exercise their right to purchase and they offered the Company the sum of £10,105, which was immediately countered by a claim for £24,000. The Corporation therefore applied to the Board of Trade for arbitration and Sir Frederick Bramwell was appointed as referee to determine the value, which was finally settled at £11,394. The deal was completed on 31st October, 1901, and the Reading Corporation Tramways came into being.

As an anti-climax to all the foregoing litigation, the Company paid back to the Corporation the sum of £49 0s. 1d. in respect of : —

    (a) the proportion of rates and taxes up to the date of transfer.

    (b) depreciation in value of stores on hand.

    (c) two horses which had died !

Photo Courtesy Walton Adams & Son, Ltd.
**Reading Tramways Company Car No. 1 as renewed about 1890.
Photo taken at corner of King's Road and Fatherson Road.**

CHAPTER II.

THE HORSE TRAMWAYS UNDER MUNICIPAL OPERATION.

The undertaking of which the Corporation now found themselves the owners was in a rather dilapidated condition. The cars were in a poor state of repair and the horses were described as having a "preponderance of rib," while the tracks left much to be desired. Of the 85 horses, 15 were found to be unfit for further work and the newly-formed Tramways Committee under its Chairman, Alderman Berkeley Monck, instructed the Manager, Mr. Groves, to obtain 20 new animals forthwith. In the short period of about 18 months during which the Corporation worked the horse tramways a total of 50 horses had to be purchased. In order that a $7\frac{1}{2}$-minute service could be provided, the Manager was authorised to obtain two or three secondhand cars, but no evidence can be found that these were in fact acquired. The cars were repainted with the words "*The Reading Corporation Tramways*" on the lower side panels, the definite article also appearing on the tickets. Fixed stopping places were introduced and 24 modern ticket punches hired, while weekly traffic returns were published in the local Press.

Complaints were constantly being made concerning alleged cruelty to the horses, one regular cause of complaint being flogging of the animals when negotiating the steep curve up to Factory Bridge. To remedy this a trace horse was stationed at the bridge to assist on the incline. The animals were also given a "rise," their allowance of corn being increased from 16 lbs. to 20 lbs. per day. Having thus improved the lot of the horses, the Tramways Committee next increased the drivers' wages from 3s. 6d. to 4s. per day. These men who worked about 70 hours a week were also given one day off in nine.

The Reading Tramways Order, 1899, as mentioned in the previous chapter, authorised construction of extensions at each end of the horse tramway, full details being as follows :—

TRAMWAY No. 1 (5 furlongs 6.6 chains in length, whereof 4 furlongs 1.8 chains will be single line and 1 furlong 4.8 chains will be double line) commencing by a junction with the existing tramway at its termination in King's Road, proceeding along King's Road across London Road along Wokingham Road and terminating in the last-named road at a point 9 yards or thereabouts measured in a north-westerly direction from the lamp column No. 404 at the junction of Wokingham Road and St. Peter's Road.

Tramway No. 1 will be single line except at the following places, where it will be double line, namely :—

(a) In King's Road, London Road and Wokingham Road for a distance of 77 yards or thereabouts measured eastwards from the commence-of the tramway.

(b) In Wokingham Road for a distance of 66 yards or thereabouts measured eastwards from a point 10 yards eastwards of the west side of Bulmershe Road.

(c) In Wokingham Road for a distance of 66 yards or thereabouts measured north-westwards from a point 110 yards northwest of the west side of Culver Road.

(d) In Wokingham Road for a distance of 66 yards or thereabouts measured north-westwards from a point 6 yards north-west of the east side of Crescent Road.

(e) In Wokingham Road for a distance of 51 yards or thereabouts measured north-westwards from the termination of the tramway as before described.

TRAMWAY No. 2 (3 furlongs 3.82 chains in length, whereof 2 furlongs 2.38 chains will be single line and 1 furlong 1.44 chains will be double line) commencing by a junction with tramway No. 1 at a point 11 yards eastwards of the commencement of that tramway, proceeding along London Road and terminating therein at a point 24 yards or thereabouts westward of the centre of the west face of the South Eastern Railway bridge in London Road.

Tramway No. 2 will be single line except at the following places where it will be double line, namely:—

(a) In London Road for a distance of 65 yards or thereabouts measured eastwards from the commencement of the tramway.

(b) In London Road for a distance of 99 yards or thereabouts measured eastwards from a point 30 yards eastwards of the east side of Cholmeley Road.

(c) In London Road for a distance of 88 yards or thereabouts measured westwards from the termination of the tramway as before described.

TRAMWAY No. 3 (2 furlongs 7 chains in length, whereof 2 furlongs 0.5 chains will be single line and 6.5 chains will be double line) commencing at a point 23 yards or thereabouts measured in a north-westerly direction from the west side of Grovelands Road West* and terminating by a junction with the existing tramway at its terminus in Oxford Road.

Tramway No. 3 will be single line except at the following places where it will be double line, namely:—

(a) For a distance of 77 yards or thereabouts measured south-eastwards from the commencement of the tramway.

(b) For a distance of 66 yards or thereabouts measured north-westwards from the west boundary wall of the Barracks.

The Order contained a clause for the protection of the War Department, prohibiting the establishment of a stop or passing place immediately outside the main gate of the Barracks, while the following sections are of interest as they affected events later in the story.

Section 13.—The promoters may, with the consent of the Board of Trade, lay down double line in lieu of single line, or single line in lieu of double line or interlaced track on any part of the tramways, provided no rail is less than 9 ft. 6 in. from the footpath.

---

* Grovelands Road West is now known as Grovelands Road.

Section 14.—Where in any road with double line there is less than 9 ft. 6 in. between the rails and the footpath, the promoters shall, if required by the Board of Trade, construct a passing place or places connecting one tramway with the other and shall, when necessary, divert traffic from one to the other.

Section 22.—The promoters may reconstruct any tramway for the time being belonging to them and make such alterations as may be necessary or expedient for working the same by mechanical power.

Unfortunately, owing to the long drawn-out negotiations in connection with the purchase of the Company, the Corporation were unable to implement the provisions of this Order as required under Section 18 of the Tramways Act, 1870, namely that substantial progress with the works authorised be made within one year of the granting of an Order, and that such works be completed within two years. It was therefore necessary to apply to the Board of Trade for the period to be prolonged, extension being granted until the 1st August, 1902, in the first instance, by which date, however, it again became necessary to further prolong the period until the 1st August, 1903.

Photo Courtesy Walton Adams & Son, Ltd.
Company Car No. 4 in Broad Street, c.1900.

Work actually commenced at the Wokingham Road terminus on 21st April, 1902, followed by the London Road branch and finally the Oxford Road extension, so that by 13th December, 1902, horse cars were running over all the extensions authorised by the 1899 Order. Here it should be noted that some variation was made (under Section 13 above) from the lines as authorised, inasmuch as double line was laid in Tramway No. 1 in lieu of single line between Sections (d) and (e), while Tramway No. 2 was laid as double line for its entire length.

20

The next step was the reconstruction and electrification of the original tramway, during which the horse car services were maintained as far as possible, the work being carried out in sections and shuttle services operated on either side of the work in progress. The horse car tracks were completely relaid as double line throughout, with the exception of the short distance under the Great Western Railway Company's bridge in Oxford Road where scant clearances made it necessary to revert to single track. In Broad Street, a third line was provided between the main tracks with facing and trailing connections thereto, to provide a lay-by for cars reversing at that point.

One rather alarming incident occurred on the 25th May, 1903, near the Cemetery Junction when the driver of a horse tram proceeding to Wokingham Road failed to notice a wire left hanging across the road by men erecting the overhead line. The wire caught beneath the chin of a lady riding on the top deck of the car, dragging her from her seat and throwing her over the side to the ground. Her fall was considerably checked by her dress catching in the side of the car and she was fortunate to suffer nothing worse than severe shock and concussion. The Contractors for the overhead work, Messrs. R. W. Blackwell, accepted responsibility and a settlement for damages was made of £150, although by agreement the Corporation paid £25 of this sum.

This was not the only untoward event during the last months of the horse cars as an account appeared in the ' Reading Standard ' of a runaway tram horse which on the 28th March, 1903, " . . . had the temerity let alone the bodily strength and vigour to make a dash for freedom. This particular quadruped," continued the report, " is, or was employed as a chain horse to assist its fellows of the cars to drag their heavy load up the hill which curves towards Factory Bridge. Cogitating in his equine mind upon the state of his kind and being like a true Briton opposed to slavery, he arrived at the conclusion that escape was possible. Accordingly the brave animal rushed off, the chains he carried clanking in chorus with the beat of his hooves. Straight down King's Road he flew, naught hindering his flight, until he turned round the corner into Minister Street. Here an ill-advised man got in the way and, surprising to relate, this excellent animal was so amazingly strong that the obstruction was unceremoniously overturned. The unstable steed pursued his mad career unchecked, unconquered and uncaught, while the man who had been rendered unconscious was taken to hospital." The gentle sarcasm of the reporter is another indication of the poor quality of the tram horses.

Yet another and more alarming experience befell some tramcar passengers on the 10th June, 1903, when a horse car driven by William Joyce was proceeding down King Street. The driver found that neither of the brakes would act and the car gathered speed down the hill forcing the horses into a gallop, along Kings Road and over Crown Bridge. Here the animals became detached from the car and bolted ahead as far as Factory Bridge where they were stopped. So great was the momentum gained by the car, that it continued horseless along King's Road past the biscuit factory and nearly mounted the bridge. The gradient stopped it however, and it ran back down the hill again as far as Watlington Street. The car was loaded but no one was hurt and no damage done.

By the beginning of July, 1903, the electric system was complete and awaited the opening which was arranged for the 22nd of that month. It was at first proposed to withdraw the horse cars on the 19th to leave a couple of days for the electric car drivers to get used to the routes, but

21

Photo—M. W. Earley's collection.

Horse tram No. 5 in Corporation livery at Pond House, Oxford Road, shortly before introduction of electric trams.

later it was found possible to continue horse operation until the 21st July, and in due course the following notice appeared:—

Reading Corporation Tramways.

Suspension of Car Services.

Notice is hereby given that the Horse Cars will cease running after Tuesday night, 21st instant, and there will be no service until about 5.0 p.m. on Wednesday, 22nd instant, when electric car services will commence.

By order.

Tramway Offices,
Mill Lane,
READING.

15th July, 1903.

Following closure, the horse car depot in Oxford Road, the cars and horses were sold by public auction. The depot became a school for defective children, but has long since disappeared, the site being occupied by shops at the present time. Of the cars, one (No. 9) is reputed to have been purchased by the Wantage Tramway Company, who ran it until 1926 as their No. 1, while others ended their days as sheds in local gardens.

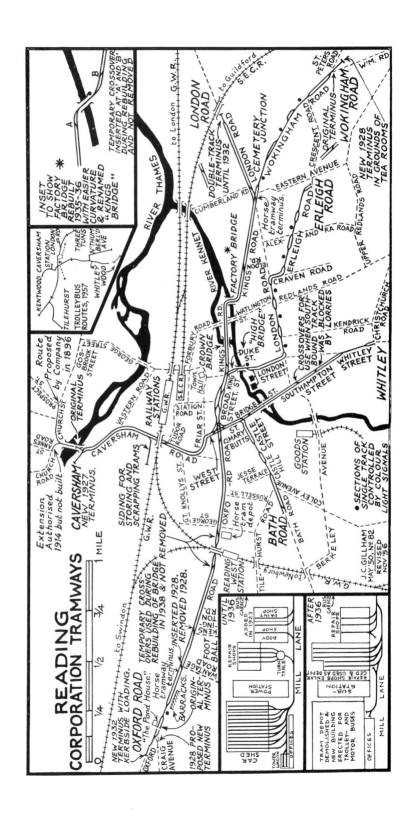

CHAPTER III.

THE ELECTRIC TRAMWAYS.

Reading had grown rapidly during the latter part of the nineteenth century and now had a population of some 70,000 living in an area which stretched well beyond the territory served by the horse tramway. It was therefore necessary to provide transport facilities in the newly developed parts of the town, and with this end in view, at a meeting of the Council on 8th January, 1900, the Mayor moved " . . . that in the judgment of this Council it is expedient for this Council to promote in the next session of Parliament, a Bill which has been deposited in Parliament under the short title of the Reading Corporation (Tramways) Bill, being a Bill to confer powers upon the Corporation of the Borough of Reading with respect to the construction and working of tramways in the Borough and for other purposes." The motion, seconded by Councillor G. W. Webb, was carried unanimously, and the Town Clerk was instructed to proceed with the matter.

The Bill was duly presented and began its slow progress through Parliament. Petitions were deposited by The Reading Gas Company, Ltd., The Great Western Railway Company, The Reading Tramways Company, Ltd., Messrs. H. & G. Simonds, Ltd. and Mrs. G. E. Cookes. The Gas Company were naturally concerned with possible interference with their pipes and mains, the railway's interest concerned the works involved in Mill Lane where the depot and power station were to be constructed on the banks of the Kennet Canal which was owned by the railway company, and the Reading Tramways Company objected to the crossing of their tracks involved at West Street junction.* Messrs. H. & G. Simonds were the owners of a large brewery situated on both sides of Bridge Street and they feared that the tramway traffic would interfere with their own wagons using that street. During the hearing of the objections, the brewers used considerable pressure, without success, to persuade the Corporation to run the Whitley tram route along Mount Pleasant to join the Erleigh Road line in London Street instead of via Southampton Street and Bridge Street. Mrs. Cookes was the owner of property in Caversham Road which she claimed would be injuriously affected. Protective clauses were inserted to satisfy the gas, and railway companies and Mrs. Cookes, the Bill then passing to the Lords on 19th June, 1900. The brewers and the Tramway Company renewed their objections in the Upper House but the Bill finally received Royal Assent on the 30th July, 1900. The tussles involved in the passage of the Bill had gone on concurrently with the litigation with the Tramways Company over purchase, and the Town Clerk must have had a very busy and trying time. The delays caused certain ratepayers to suggest that while the legal experts were arguing and Reading was not getting its tramways, horse buses should be run over the proposed tram routes, but this did not materialise.

---

* The horse tramway was not yet Corporation property.

The lines authorised by the Act were as follows:—

TRAMWAY No. 1 (6 furlongs 1.12 chains in length, whereof 4.82 chains will be single line and 5 furlongs 6.3 chains will be double line) commencing at a point 7 yards or thereabouts measured in a north-westerly direction from the pump in Whitley Street at its junction with Christchurch Road proceeding along Whitley Street, Southampton Street, Bridge Street and St Mary's Butts and terminating therein at a point opposite the north end of the public conveniences.

TRAMWAY No. 2 (a double line 1 furlong 0.1 chain in length) commencing by a junction with Tramway No. 1 at its termination in St. Mary's Butts, proceeding along St. Mary's Butts across Broad Street and the existing tramways and terminating in West Street at a point 9 yards or thereabouts measured in a north-westerly direction from the south-west corner of the Vine Hotel in Broad Street.

TRAMWAY No. 2A (a single line 1.36 chains in length) commencing by a junction with Tramway No. 2 at a point 33 yards or thereabouts measured in a south-easterly direction from its termination in West Street and terminating by a junction with the existing tramways at a point 23 yards or thereabouts measured in an easterly direction from a point at the intersection of the imaginary centre lines of Broad Street and West Street.

TRAMWAY N.o 2B (a double line 1.1 chains in length) commencing by a junction with tramway No. 2 at its termination in West Street and terminating in Broad Street at a point 15 yards or thereabouts measured in an easterly direction from the point of intersection of the imaginary centre lines of West Street and Broad Street.

TRAMWAY No. 3 (6 furlongs 2.09 chains in length whereof 2 chains will be single line and 6 furlongs 0.9 chain will be double line) commencing by a junction with Tramway No. 2 at its termination in West Street and proceeding along West Street, Friar Street and Caversham Road and terminating in the last-mentioned road at a point 2 yards or thereabouts south of the intersection of the imaginary centre lines of the River Thames tow path and Caversham Road.

TRAMWAY No. 4 (4 furlongs 3.75 chains in length whereof 1 furlong 2.94 chains will be single line and 3 furlongs 0.81 chain will be double line) commencing in Bath Road at a point 200 yards or thereabouts measured in a westerly direction from the intersection of the imaginary centre lines of Bath Road and Coley Avenue and proceeding along Bath Road, Castle Hill and Castle Street and terminating in St. Mary's Butts by a junction with tramway No. 2 at its commencement.

TRAMWAY No. 5 (1 mile 2 furlongs 1.36 chains in length whereof 5 furlongs 4.75 chains will be single line and 4 furlongs 6.61 chains will be double line) commencing by a junction with the existing tramway in King Street at a point 16 yards or thereabouts measured in a westerly direction from a point at the intersection of the imaginary centre lines of King's Road and Duke Street proceeding along Duke Street over the River Kennet by High Bridge along London Street, London Road, Craven Road and Erleigh Road and terminating in the last-mentioned road at a point 9 yards or thereabouts measured in a northerly direction from a point at the intersection of the imaginary centre lines of Addington Road and Erleigh Road.

TRAMWAY No. 6 (a single line 7.4 chains in length) commencing at a point 10 yards or thereabouts measured in a south westerly direction from the entrance door at the south-west front of St. Giles Mill (old part) in Mill Lane, proceeding along Mill Lane and terminating in London Street by a junction with tramway No. 5 at a point 15 yards or thereabouts measured in a southerly direction from a public lamp at the corner of London Street and Mill Lane.

TRAMWAY NO. 6A (a single line 1.19 chains in length) commencing at a junction with tramway No. 6 at a point in Mill Lane 16 yards or thereabouts measured in a westerly direction from the public lamp at the junction of London Street and Mill Lane and terminating in London Street by a junction with tramway No. 5 at a point 16 yards or thereabouts measured in a northerly direction from the said lamp.

Briefly summarising the foregoing, tramways Nos. 1, 2 and 3 comprised the Whitley to Caversham route which was double line except for the short length in Whitley Street and the Caversham terminal stub. Tramway No. 4, the Bath Road branch, was double track from the terminus to Jesse Terrace then single to St. Mary's Butts with one passing place at Boarded Lane. The Erleigh Road route was No. 5 which left the existing tramway at Duke Street junction and at once became single track over High Bridge. This bridge, which in recent years has been scheduled as an ancient monument, was built in 1787 and is regarded as a particularly handsome structure by those with an eye for such things, but the local police and traffic authorities have other views, as the steep " hump-back " and narrowness of the bridge make it a serious obstacle to traffic flow. Once over the bridge, the tramway resumed double line as far as the junction of London Street and London Road, whence single line continued all the way to Erleigh Road terminus broken only by passing loops at Kendrick Road, Albion Place, Craven Road, Alexandra Road and DeBeauvoir Road.

Tramways 6 and 6A together formed the depot connection in Mill Lane, but No. 6 was not built in its entirety, the curve leading from Mill Lane in the Erleigh Road direction being omitted. Tramways 2A and 2B were the connecting curves of the West Street junction and it should be noted that No. 2A was laid as double line, not single as authorised, certain

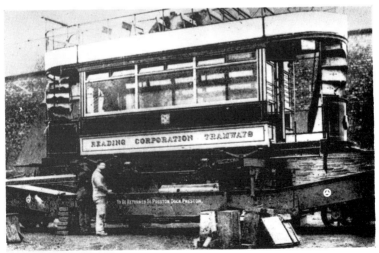

Reading Corporation tramcar en route from makers, 1903.

27

clauses of the 1899 Order, including No. 13, being also applicable to the 1900 Act. The total route mileage of the electric tramways was 7.45, of which 5.75 miles were double track.

As soon as the Bill received Royal Assent, steps were taken to obtain tenders for the various sections of the work involved, contracts being awarded in due course to the following firms :—

Messrs. E. Nuttall, Trafford Park—Track.

Messrs. R. W. Blackwell & Co.—Overhead, Power Station and Car Sheds.

Messrs. Dick Kerr & Co.—Rolling stock.

Messrs. Nuttall established a depot and dump for materials in Great Knollys Street, Reading, and after completing conversion of the horse car tracks, turned their attention to the other routes. Several difficulties were encountered during the work, not the least of which was the wholesale pilfering of wooden paving blocks which went on, certain unscrupulous inhabitants having discovered that these made excellent fuel. A few prosecutions put a stop to this trouble, however. Another delay was caused by a strike of labourers who demanded higher pay, but there was no shortage of labour at the time and many men were found willing to do the work for the same pay and the strike was broken.

The permanent way consisted of steel rails rolled by Messrs. Belckow, Vaughan and Co., Ltd., of Middlesbrough weighing 96 lb. per yard and laid in 45 feet lengths on 6 in. of 4 to 1 concrete. Rails were 7 in. deep and had a 7 in. base flange with a 7/16 in. web. The tread was $1\frac{7}{8}$ in. in width and the groove $1\frac{1}{8}$ in. wide and of the same depth. 2 ft. 7 in. fishplates were used in connection with welded joints, eight bolts being used at each joint. A pair of fishplates weighed 76 lb. The rails were laid to a gauge of 4 ft. with tie bars every six feet. The usual electrical bonds were provided at each joint together with cross bonds every 120 feet. Paving varied according to the location, three methods being used, viz. :—

(a) Granite Setts	9 in. x 4 in. x 5 in.	
(b) Basaltic Lava Setts	9 in. x 4 in. x 5 in.	
(c) Yellow Deal Blocks (creosoted).	9 in. x 3 in. x 5 in.	

The wood blocks were laid with a " teething " row of Jarrah hardwood blocks to prevent ruts wearing near the rails. Distributor cables were laid in conduits with Sykes patent drawing-in boxes every 65 yards.

Special work at junctions and the car shed fan were made by the Lorain Steel Company of Philadelphia, U.S.A., a fact which caused much dissention in the Council Chamber at the time. The laying of West Street junction necessitated the complete closure of this busy crossroads and in order to minimise inconvenience the work was carried on continuously for 24 hours per day. The track had been assembled and tested in America and when laid in Reading was found to fit perfectly.

The steepest gradient on the system was 1 in 16 for short distances on the bridges over the Kennet, but the 1 in 21 of Southampton Street on the Whitley route was the steepest incline of appreciable length, resulting in this route being known among the staff as " up and down the bump." Curves were generally limited to a radius of 40 feet, but at Craven Road corner on the Erleigh Road route it was found necessary to adopt a radius of 37 feet. All trackwork was completed by the first week of March, 1903, at a total cost of £92,000.

Erection of the overhead involved planting some 570 31 ft. standards, which were sunk 6 ft. 6 in. in the ground at 40-yard intervals and embedded in concrete. Trolley wire was of 0000 S.W.G. hard drawn copper, suspended partly from side poles with bracket arms and partly from centre poles on the bow-string principle. Centre poles were situated as follows:—

Oxford Road (G.W.R. bridge)– Duke Street.

Factory Bridge   —Cemetery Junction.

London Street (Queens Road)—London Street (top).

West Street (Friar Street)   —St. Mary's Butts (Castle Street).

Jesse Terrace   —Bath Road Terminus.

Caversham Terminus   —Vastern Road.

The usual ornamental bases and finials were provided, the bases embodying the Borough Arms. Centre poles were painted white with green bases and side poles light green with the bases a darker shade of the same colour. At section insulators, a white band was painted on the poles with a large red spot thereon. Frogs on the overhead line were originally hand pulled by cords, but later automatic turning was adopted by means of drop levers actuated by passing trolley poles. A proposal was put forward that electric street lighting should be introduced on the tram routes, using tramway standards and current from the overhead line, but technical difficulties prevented the adoption of this idea.

The overhead contractor was also responsible for the erection of the depot on the site of the old St. Giles Mill in Mill Lane, the demolition of which was closely watched by local antiquarians in the hope that ancient

Photo—R. B. Parr collection.

Car No. 4 on Caversham to Whitley route at West Street junction, 1903. Note centre pole method of overhead suspension.

relics might be brought to light, as the site was that of the original Saxon settlement at Reading over 1,000 years previously. Nothing of great interest was found, however. The power station equipment consisted of three Babcock and Willcox water tube boilers with superheaters and Underfeed stokers, supplying steam to four Browett and Lindley compound vertical engines, each of which drove a British Westinghouse 6 pole, compound type dynamo of 100 Kw., giving a total output of 400 Kw. The 150 feet high chimney stack was a familiar landmark in the centre of Reading until its demolition in 1938. Current at 500 volts was supplied to the line through a switchboard in the main power station building.

The car shed adjoined the power station and consisted of a brick shed containing ten roads totalling over 700 yards of track, with a sunken floor providing inspection pits under all roads. Two further roads were added in a separate bay on the east side of the shed following the arrival of additional cars in 1904; these latter roads were not provided with pits. Well equipped repair, machine and paint shops were provided, access to some of which was by means of a turntable. On the extreme eastern side of the site was a permanent way yard, but this was later built over to provide garage accommodation when the Corporation commenced to operate motor buses in 1919.

One feature which calls for some explanation is the fact that no direct physical connection existed between the depot and the Whitley route in Southampton Street a mere 100 yards away, cars from Whitley to depot having to travel nearly ¾ mile via Broad Street and Duke Street. The reason was that in the early days, Mill Lane did not exist as a made up road but was merely a rough tow path along the mill stream. This stream was subsequently built over and now flows beneath the widened Mill Lane.

Rolling stock at the opening of the electric tramways consisted of 30 four-wheeled cars supplied by Dick, Kerr & Co. of Preston, with bodies by the Electric Railway and Tramway Works, Ltd. These cars were 27 feet long, and seated 22 inside and 28 on the top deck. Interior seating was longitudinal, covered with carpeting easily removable for cleaning, and embodying the letters " R.C.T." woven into the pattern, but this was removed after a few years and the seats left as plain wood. The lower saloons had three side windows, each fitted with spring roller blinds and the interior finish was in quartered oak. Reversed stairs led to the upper deck where seating was of the usual wooden slat reversible type, arranged with pairs on one side of the gangway and single seats on the other, reversing midway where the trolley standard was placed centrally. Decency boards were provided round the top decks with railings and wire mesh above.

The cars were carried on Brill 21E type trucks with two 25 h.p. DK.25A motors driving 30 in. wheels. Controllers were type DB1, form B. Tidswell lifeguards were provided, and the cars were conveyed to Reading by rail, fully painted and assembled, with the exception of trolley standards and other top deck fittings which would have fouled the railway loading gauge. Livery was lake (officially described as " claret ") and cream, waist panels, dashes, staircases, cantrails, trolley standards, trucks and lifeguards being lake and rocker panels, window frames and decency boards cream, although the last named were soon let as advertising space and subsequently appeared cream for short periods only, when spaces became temporarily vacant. Top deck seats were painted a medium brown while the railings and wire mesh were black as were the car buffers. Lining out was gold on the lake parts and black on the cream with a fine red line inside the black. Numbers, which were of course 1 to 30, and the words " Reading Corporation Tram-ways " on the rocker panels, were in gold, shaded blue. Small gold arrows were placed on the canopy ends with the words " Turn trolley this way," but later the words were omitted. The trolley poles, which were fitted with swivel heads, were turned by means of a rope, and early photographs show the cars running with this rope dangling over the end of the car and tied loosely to a handrail, but this was soon altered and the trailing end of the rope was tied to the bottom end of the boom. All trolley turning could then be done from the top deck, for which purpose additional arrows were painted on the trolley standards to indicate the direction of turning. On running into depot, the ropes were always untied and thrown over the end of the cars as conductors had to walk behind holding the rope to " juggle " trolleys through the several dummy frogs in the depot yard.

Destination indicators of roller blind pattern were fitted at each end of the top deck above the railings. It was originally suggested that the blinds should bear the indications—Caversham Road, Oxford Road, Bath Road, Erleigh Road, Whitley, Broad Street, London Road, Wokingham Road, King's Road and FULL! The last two were not adopted, however, and in their place Cemetery Junction, Kensington Road, Special and Car Sheds were added. One is tempted to wonder if it would have been part of the conductor's duty to turn the indicators to "Full" each time the car became loaded to capacity. On each side of the cars a pair of small wooden boards was carried showing both termini simultaneously and thus these did not require changing while the car remained on one route, but in the case of the Erleigh Road-Caversham-Whitley triangular service, chang-ing was of course necessary at each terminus. It was found that rough and careless handling of the boards caused damage to the paintwork of the cars, so in September, 1911, boxes containing roller blinds were substituted, attached to the inside of the centre windows.

Photo Courtesy E. Phillips, Long Beach, Calif., U.S.A.
Car No. 19 in original condition at Bath Road terminus c.1908. Note side destination boards.

31

Lattice folding gates were provided to the platforms, but these were removed at an early date and replaced by chains. Shortly before the cars were delivered, the 'Reading Standard' dated 4th April, 1903, contained a beautifully executed line drawing of a tramcar by a local artist, Mr. H. T. Morley, headed "What Reading Trams will Look Like." Actually the artist had used as a model a car supplied by Dick, Kerr & Co. to Birkenhead Corporation which differed from the Reading cars in a number of respects, chief of which were the half-turn normal stairs and a Peckham Cantilever truck. The word "Reading" had been substituted for "Birkenhead" on the rocker panel and altogether the picture was an interesting case of what might have been.

Mr. Groves, who had managed the horse tramways, was not an engineer and it therefore became necessary to advertise for a new manager. The salary offered was £300 per annum and there were 120 applicants for the post. The successful candidate was Mr. Walter Binns, A.M.I.E.E., who had previously been Senior Engineer of the Newcastle-upon-Tyne Corporation Tramways. His chief assistant at Reading was Mr. A. G. Shearer who came from the Cork Electric Lighting and Tramways Company, where he had been Engineer in Charge. Mr. Groves took the position of Traffic Superintendent.

Trial trips were first run over the electric tramways on 8th July, 1903, with car No. 11, and thereafter the Erleigh Road section was in daily use for training motormen. It is of interest to recall that thirty-two years later, the same section was used to train trolleybus drivers on a specially erected length of overhead.

On the 14th July, 1903, the Board of Trade Inspector, Lt.-Col. von Donop and Mr. E. P. Trotter, the Board's Electrical Advisor, carried out an inspection of the entire system. Accompanied by the Mayor, the Town Clerk, the Borough Surveyor, Mr. John Bowen, who had planned the tramways and the Consulting Electrical Engineer, Mr. Winslow, together with representatives of the Contractors concerned, they started from Broad Street "loop" in two special tramcars travelling first to Oxford Road. Wokingham Road was next visited, the cars then returning to Cemetery Junction where reversal took place for the run to London Road terminus. Returning to Broad Street, one car then proceeded to Bath Road and back to St. Mary's Butts, but as there was no convenient cross-over here, the party changed to the other car which was waiting on the outward track and proceeded to Whitley. Next came Caversham Road with a prolonged stop at the railway bridge for the Inspector to make careful measurements of clearances. It had at first been thought it would be necessary to work this route with single-deck cars, but it had been found that double-deck cars could be used if the road were to be lowered a few inches. This had been done, but here and also at the Oxford Road railway bridge the Inspector required large warning signs to be affixed to the bridges requesting top deck passengers to "Keep your seats." A suggestion was made, unofficially, for the fixing of tassels on brackets two or three feet out from the side of the bridge, which would brush against anyone standing up on the tops of cars and warn them to lower their heads, but the idea was not adopted! It was these bridges which prevented the use of top-covered cars in Reading.

The inspection was completed by a journey to Erleigh Road following which permission was given for public services to commence. Total capital expenditure on the electric tramways amounted to £223,000.

Ceremonial opening day procession of trams leaving Mill Lane depot
22nd July, 1903.   Alderman A. H. Bull driving Car No. 1.

CHAPTER IV.

FROM ELECTRIFICATION TO THE FIRST WORLD WAR.

Wednesday, the 22nd July, 1903, the day fixed for the opening of the Reading Corporation Electric Tramways, was undoubtedly a very eventful one for the Borough. The Mayor, Alderman A. H. Bull, was serving his third consecutive year in that office, it being generally understood that the prospect of the opening of the system had been the principal factor in inducing Mr. Bull to accept the honour for the third time. A distinguished gathering assembled at the Town Hall where, at 1.30 p.m., some 300 guests sat down to luncheon, to the accompaniment of an organ recital and violin solos. Many fine speeches were made and the Borough Member, Mr. G. W. Palmer, proposed "Success to the Reading Corporation Tramways Undertaking," to which the Mayor made a suitable reply.

After the repast the whole assembly proceeded to the Tramways Depot where, at 3.30 p.m., the Mayoress switched on the current and formally declared the tramways open. A procession of ten cars then left the depot in numerical order, No. 1 driven by the Mayor, followed by Nos. 2 and 3 all suitably decorated with ferns and flags and bearing the more important personages. Nos. 4 to 10 followed with the lesser-known guests and without the decorative embellishments. The procession ran first to Oxford Road, where there must have been considerable difficulty in managing the convoy on the single-track section, as there was certainly not enough room at the terminus to accommodate all ten cars at one time. The turn round accomplished, however, they then proceeded to Wokingham Road and back to Broad Street where the distinguished passengers alighted. Immediately an enormous throng surged around the cars, everyone trying to achieve the distinction of being the first fare-paying passenger. Services began on all routes simultaneously and up to a very late hour all cars were packed for every journey; even then many were disappointed and had to go home without having had a ride. A total of £65 was taken in fares during the evening.

It is difficult today to appreciate what an immense improvement the change-over from horse to electric traction represented, and it is interesting to record that the local Press printed a long article on the tramways and issued a special art supplement of photographs to commemorate the occasion.

Traffic for the first seven complete days was as follows:—

Thursday	23/7/03	£80	3s.	0d.	with	16	cars running.
Friday	24/7/03	£108	0s.	0d.	,,	18	,, ,,
Saturday	25/7/03	£139	15s.	0d.	,,	20	,, ,,
Sunday	26/7/03	£105	14s.	0d.	,,	20	,, ,,
Monday	27/7/03	£90	10s.	0d.	,,	20	,, ,,

Tuesday   28/7/03   £80   1s.   0d.   ,,   21 cars running.

Wednesday   29/7/03   £90   1s.   0d.   ,,   22   ,,   ,,

Thereafter 22 cars were employed Mondays to Fridays, 26 on Saturdays and 24 on Sundays. Basic services operated from the opening were:—

Oxford Road—Wokingham Road	every	10	minutes.
Oxford Road—London Road	,,	10	,,
Caversham —Whitley	,,	9	,,
Caversham —Erleigh Road	,,	16	,,
Bath Road —Erleigh Road	,,	16	,,

The foregoing services began at 7.45 a.m., and in addition workmen's cars ran from about 5.30 a.m. from outer termini at 15-30 minute intervals. Midday and evening peak hour extras were also provided. Last through cars, terminus to terminus left at about 10.55 p.m. and last cars termini to depot at 11.25 p.m. Sunday services which commenced at 2.0 p.m. were similar except that there was no service to London Road, while during the winter months the Erleigh Road-Bath Road service was suspended on Sundays except for a skeleton service between Erleigh Road and Broad Street only, after 5.30 p.m., primarily for the benefit of people attending places of worship. Complaints were received from time to time from local clergy regarding the noise made by tramcars, and a request was actually made that the running of cars should be suspended during the hours of divine service. This was not acceded to, but a standing instruction was issued to all motormen to drive as quietly as possible past places of worship. There was, incidentally, an Annual Church Parade of Tramway-men in the early years but the practice died out, probably during the Great War.

In the light of operating experience, services underwent a number of changes in the first year or so, the first alteration being the suspension of the Caversham-Erleigh Road service during the winter of 1903-4; but as from 15th February, 1904, it was restored when the following arrangement was introduced:—

Oxford Road—Wokingham Road	every	10	minutes.
Oxford Road—London Road	,,	10	,,
Bath Road —Broad Street	,,	10	,,
Caversham —Whitley	,,	15	,,
Caversham —Erleigh Road	,,	15	,,
Erleigh Road—Whitley	,,	15	,,

The last three services mentioned were worked as a triangular service providing a 7½-minute frequency on each leg. From April, 1904, all cars from Oxford Road ran to Wokingham Road (every 5 minutes) and Bath Road cars were extended to London Road (every 10 minutes), while on Sundays during the summer of 1904 a Bath Road-Caversham service was tried.

At last a satisfactory method of operating seemed to have been found and services remained as described for many years. The Oxford Road-Wokingham Road route became known as the " main line " and all the other routes as the " side roads."

The Fare Table in force from the opening was as follows:—

Main Line 1d. stages.

Oxford Road terminus—West Street Juncion.
West Street Junction —Wokingham Road or London Road.
Western Elms Avenue —Fatherson Road.

2d. stages.

Oxford Road terminus —Wokingham Road or London Road.

Side Roads 1d. stages.

Caversham terminus	—Whitley terminus.
Erleigh Road	—Broad Street.
Bath Road	—Crown Street.
Caversham	—Crown Street.

2d. stages.

Bath Road	—Erleigh Road.
Caversham	—Erleigh Road.

Workmen's 1d. Return Tickets were issued on all cars up to 7.45 a.m., available for any distance and for return on day of issue only between the hours of 5.30 and 6.30 p.m. (Mondays-Fridays) or before 1.30 p.m. Saturdays. As from 3rd December, 1903, the return availability (Mondays-Fridays) was extended to any time on day of issue. During a discussion on fares in the Council Chamber just prior to the opening of the tramways one member asked if Workmen's fares would be available to women, and in reply (amid laughter) it was stated, " Yes to anyone, to the Mayor if he so wished." Transfer tickets were not issued although from time to time during the life of the tramways requests for this facility were made, always unsuccessfully. Special prepaid tickets were sold in bulk to the Post Office for use by postmen delivering the mail, but these were covered by a contract. The full range of tickets consisted originally of eight types as under : —

Ordinary	...	...	1d.
Ordinary	...	...	2d.
Workmen's	...	...	1d.
Scholar's	...	...	$\frac{1}{2}$d.
Postman's	...	...	1d.
Prepaid	...	...	1d. (no discount).
Parcels	...	...	1d.
Exchange	...	...	— (issued in exchange for Workmen's, Prepaids, etc.)

Sixty ticket punches were hired from the Ticket Punch and Register Co., Ltd., but from about 1911, when the original contract expired, all punches were supplied by Alfred Williamson and Co. Tickets were printed by the Punch and Ticket Co., Ltd.

For a considerable period following the opening of the system, the ' Reading Standard ' carried a weekly column headed " The Electric Tramways—Items of Interest," and also printed a considerable number of readers' letters full of advice on how to run tramways ! In the issue dated 5th September, 1903, we read, " . . . not much to record this week. There is the usual big batch of suggestions and the usual small batch of complaints—the former for the most part altogether lacking in originality and the latter altogether lacking serious grounds." One irate correspondent, who had been left behind by a tramcar, wrote, " Would it not be well to make the appointment of motormen dependent upon a simple side sight test? Being desirous the other evening of boarding an east-bound car I planted myself within two feet of the rails immediately opposite the pole and held up my right hand. This, not having the desired effect, I held up everything I possessed of a liftable character, and then still noting an absence of response, began to execute a sword dance and to wave my hat, umbrella and parcels about in a manner which must have been highly amusing to watchers on. Notwithstanding all this the car passed me without slackening speed, and on the face of the controlling official was a look of stony superiority which struck me as being exaggerated even for an electric car driver in a brand new uniform!" The editor's comment following this was, " We cannot help thinking that our correspondent was mistaken for one of the numerous fraternity which, for some obscure reason, makes a collection of tram tickets!"

Considerable trouble was experienced with broken axles during the first few months of operation, at one period no less than eleven cars being laid up with this defect. The position became so serious that a special report was called for and after investigation by experts it was decided that the trouble was primarily due to unnecessarily deep penetration of the axles when cutting the keyways for securing the gears, all breakages having occurred at this point. A secondary cause was thought to be a slight variation from gauge in one or two places in the Lorain special trackwork. The makers replaced the axles of the entire fleet without charge.

A Parcels Delivery Service was introduced shortly after the electric cars commenced running, operated by Parcels Agents who were tradesmen with premises situated at various points along the tramway routes. These Agents accepted parcels to be forwarded by tramcar, and received and delivered within reasonable distance of their premises parcels brought by car from other agents. They were paid commission for their services. The scale of charges for the parcels service was as follows :—

For parcels carried by car to Agents and
left until called for—not exceeding 7 lb. ...   ...   1d.

    do.   not exceeding 28 lb. ...   ...   2d.

For parcels delivered to any address
within ½ mile of agents' premises—

            not exceeding 7 lb. ...   ...   2d.

    do.   not exceeding 28 lb. ...   ...   3d.

In 1904, the only addition to the tramcar fleet was made in the shape of six bogie cars, Nos. 31 to 36, and a water car which took number 37. These were ordered in February from Dick, Kerr & Co., Ltd. and were delivered in July just in time for the August Bank Holiday traffic. The eight-wheeled cars were carried on Brill 22E maximum traction trucks and powered by DK6A motors each of 35 h.p.; controllers were Type DB1 form C. These cars were 33 ft. 6 in. in length and seated 30 inside and 40 on the top deck, access to which was by means of half turn normal stairs. Interior seating was 2 and 1 transverse, and on the top deck 2 and 2, with the exception of the middle pair of seats which was 1 and 1 to clear the trolley standard. There were also curved seats for 3 on each canopy. A bulkhead lamp on a standard was situated at the top of each stairway. Interior finish was in polished oak and crimson-coloured blinds were provided to side windows of which there were five. Electric bells were provided at first but were later replaced by cord-operated ones.

The first trial run with a bogie car was made on 29th July, 1904, presumably with No. 31, when Councillors and their wives made a tour for which the car was specially fitted with carpets and easy chairs! The bogie cars were used throughout their lives on the main line and it was only on rare special occasions that they appeared on the side roads. The

Photo—Author's collection.

Bogie Car No. 35 at Oxford Road terminus about 1910. The cylindrical object between the bogie trucks houses the starting resistances. Motorman is the author's father, " Tim " Jordan.

author has no personal experience of seeing them on the Bath Road or Erleigh Road sections.

The water car arrived by rail at the G.W.R. goods yard in Vastern Road on 9th September, 1904, whence it was hauled over the cobblestones by a team of seven horses to the adjacent tramway track in Caversham Road. It was a four-wheeled vehicle on a Brill 21E truck, and was equipped with a large rectangular water tank. For rail grinding, carborundum blocks were fitted between the wheels in the position of track brake blocks, and were screwed down into contact with the rails by means of a handwheel mounted on the handbrake shaft. No. 37 was known to the staff as " the watercart " and as its activities as a railgrinder took place mostly at night after regular car services had finished, many inhabitants of Reading were unaware of its existence. On the rare occasions when it did venture forth in daylight it created quite a stir among the public. A small open wagon and a tar boiler wagon were also provided for permanent way purposes and these were towed by No. 37, which incidentally was fitted with large wedge shaped snow ploughs at each end.

Mention of snow makes this a convenient point at which to describe a rather unusual Christmas Greeting Card which is in the author's possession. It consists of a photograph of a Reading tramcar, snowbound on the Bath Road route on the 25th April, 1908 which of course was rather late in the year for such a heavy fall. A copy of this card is understood to have been given to each tramway employee by the Mayor of Reading at Christmas, 1908.

It was the practice at times of heavy snowfall to operate one or two " ghost " trams all night to keep track and points clear, and it was while engaged on this duty many years ago that the following incident befell the author's father. On arriving at the Caversham terminus in the small hours of the morning a very distressed gentleman approached and explained that

Photo Courtesy W. A. Camwell.

Water Car No. 37.

he was the owner of certain business premises in the town and had just received a telephone message informing him that his property was on fire. His only means of transport at that hour of the morning was to walk through the blizzard and one can image his surprise and relief to find a tram waiting for him. He was immediately told to " jump on " and away through the deserted and snow-covered streets sped the car on what was probably the strangest journey ever performed by a Reading tram.

The first complete financial year of operation, ending on 31st March, 1905, resulted in a revenue of £32,650 from 8,018,428 passengers, and a net profit of £2,923. This net profit remained fairly constant during the first few years being £2,915 for 1905-6; £3,061 for 1906-7; £3,396 for 1907-8 and £3,390 in 1908-9. Advertisements had been placed on the cars since December, 1904, for the privilege of which the contractors, Messrs. Griffiths and Millington, paid the sum of £950 per annum. While on the subject of finance, costs and prices ruling at this time for various articles used by the tramways department give considerable food for thought to present-day readers. Coal was 9s. 3d. per ton, motormen's overcoats 20s. 6d. each, trousers 8s. 10d. per pair and caps 2s. 8d. each. The Chief Clerk's salary was £120 per annum, while a passenger who refused to pay a fare was summoned and fined 1s. including costs. Wages paid to motormen and conductors (1909) were as follows :—

Conductors—Probationers	...	...	4½d. per hour.		
Class 2	...	...	...	4¾d.	,, ,,
Class 3	...	...	...	5d.	,, ,,
Motormen —Probationers	...	...	5½d.	,, ,,	
Class 2	...	...	...	5¾d.	,, ,,
Class 3	...	...	...	6d.	,, ,,

The above rates were in respect of a basic week of 65 hours. A quarterly bonus system was in operation under which motormen, by running their cars to time and free from accidents, with economical and efficient driving and maintaining a proper observation for passengers, and providing they worked for at least 70 days per quarter, could earn a bonus of 5s. Any motorman who earned four consecutive bonuses was entitled to a further 10s. making a total possible bonus of 30s. per year. Conductors also qualified for bonus at the same rate if "their average receipts per car mile were equal to or more than the average receipts per car mile over the section on which they had worked during that quarter." The system was divided into two sections, the main line and side roads, and normally crews remained on the same section all the time, the main line being regarded as senior. The method of assessing the conductors' entitlement to bonus seems rather complicated and indeed a little unfair, as they could hardly be held entirely responsible for the amount of traffic they carried. Considerable office work must have been needed to keep individual records for each man and it was probably in view of this that the condition for conductors was later altered to " provided he complies with the Regulations of the Department, particularly with regard to observation for and courtesy to passengers, and proper collection and recording of fares."

In connection with the grading system, the men were awarded small brass conduct "stars" which were worn on their tunic sleeves to denote their class, together with discs bearing the letter "C" or "M" (conductor or motorman). In addition each man wore his number in brass numerals on his epaulettes and brass buttons on the uniform bore the town's Arms, as did the cap badge. There was a considerable amount of brass to be cleaned, and cleaned it was, the writer well remembering his father's frequent sessions with button-stick and brasso! One cannot but regret that these items do not now form part of a bus crew's equipment, and it is a sad but undeniable fact that the present-day hatless and tieless crews leave much to be desired in the way of smartness. There is no bonus scheme in force today, which is regretable, as in the old days failure to earn a bonus for three consecutive quarters caused a man to be reduced to the next lower class with corresponding loss of pay. On gaining the next bonus, however, he was restored to his former grade.

The General Manager's Report for 1909 contained one or two interesting points. On the subject of accidents, he said, " . . . it is satisfactory to be able to again report that there have been no fatal accidents or any accidents of a serious nature throughout the year. Unfortunately there are still a considerable number of accidents to passengers who insist on getting off cars whilst in motion and of the 82 passengers who fell from cars last year, 44 were ladies, 22 gentlemen, 10 boys and 6 girls." When one considers the long skirts fashionable at this time, it is surprising that ladies risked jumping off a moving car, but certainly not surprising that they should come to grief in doing so. However, the cars bore warnings against this dangerous practice and those who indulged in it did so at their own risk. Incidentally the amount paid out in Third Party Compensation for the year was only £5 12s. 7d. which, said the manager, " I venture to think must be a record for any tramway system." He continued, however, " I may remind you (the Tramways Committee) that the Department is not insured either against third party risks or employer's liability and that the Insurance Fund amounts to only £898. The accidents which have occurred during recent years on tramway systems—some of them not far from Reading have demonstrated in a convincing manner the great expense to which tramway authorities are liable through accidents which may occur."

From the report we learn that considerable trouble was being experienced with the track in King's Road between Fatherson Road and Cemetery

Junction, which was in process of being relaid. It would appear that the trouble was in the foundations and not in the actual rails, as these had only been in use six years and could hardly have been worn out. Single line working was in operation while the work was being carried out. The manager also stated that he had personally inspected the overhead wires which on the whole were in a satisfactory state, but those in Broad Street which were subject to most wear had been renewed.

During the first few years of the electric trams the internal combustion engine had developed rapidly and motor cars were appearing on the roads in ever-increasing numbers. A sign of the times occurred in May, 1909, when the Town Clerk received a letter from the Motor Union of Great Britain and Ireland, stating that the Union had been informed that the tramway poles standing in the carriageways in the Borough constituted a source of danger to the public and enquiring whether the Corporation would consider the question of removing them. No resolution was adopted in regard to the matter at the time, but the question was to recur, of which more anon.

In June, 1909, the Royal Counties Agricultural Show was held in Prospect Park, Reading and, during the four days of the Show, the number of passengers carried on the cars was 116,309, receipts amounting to £563 0s. 8d. All of the cars were in use providing additional services on all routes including a special service from Broad Street to Bath Road on which the normal fare of 1d. was specially raised to 2d., notwithstanding the fact that the Bath Road terminus was a considerable distance from the showground, so visitors had quite a long walk after leaving the cars.

The chronicles of 1909 can be brought to a close by recording three items which today may strike one as rather curious. Firstly the manager was empowered to arrange for collecting boxes to be placed on the cars during the 14 days preceding Christmas Day " for the reception of any amounts which passengers travelling on the tramways may like to contribute towards the employee's Social Club Fund." The second item was the suggestion by the local branch of the St. John Ambulance Brigade that ambulance boxes should be affixed to the tramway poles, to which the Committee would not agree. Finally the car shed at the depot was let to candidates for the forthcoming General Election, for the purpose of electioneering meetings. This brought in a substantial revenue and started a series of such lettings for various purposes, including boxing contests and at Christmas times to the G.P.O. for handling the extra mail.

A system of route indicator lights was introduced in January, 1910, bullseye lenses for the purpose being inserted in the staircase side sheets of the cars, in a position just above the driver's head. The colours adopted were as follows : —

Wokingham Road	Red
Oxford Road	Red
London Road	Green
Bath Road	Blue
Erleigh Road	Violet
Whitley	White
Caversham	Orange

The different colours were obtained by a set of coloured glass discs arranged fanwise, any one of which could be set in front of the lamp as required. It will be noted that the indication for both Wokingham Road and Oxford Road was red, which resulted in cars on this route displaying a red light

41

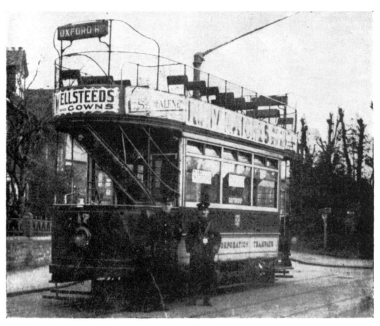

Photo—Author's collection.

**Car No. 17 with Motorman Jordan at Wokingham Road terminus
c.1911.   Note colour light route indicator.**

both front and rear. This was both confusing to intending passengers and
dangerous, as for example with a car stationary on a single track section at
night there was no clear indication to other traffic as to which way it was
travelling. This practice lasted until January, 1929, when the red route
light was altered to a rather unsatisfactory blue and white "quartered"
aspect. This appeared plain white above a distance of about 10 yards due
to the bullseye glass.

The Parcels Delivery service had not been a complete success, and for
the year 1910 the total of parcels handled by Agents was only 3,586. In
January, 1911, therefore, a new system was introduced dispensing with
Agents, whereby parcels could be handed to conductors of cars for convey·
ance to a Central Parcels Office in Broad Street, whence they were delivered
by boys riding on the cars or on bicycles to any address within half a mile
of the tramways. Parcels were also accepted for delivery to the railway
stations for despatch "rail charges forward." The new scale of charges
was : —

Not exceeding 7 lb. ...	...	...	...	1d.
Over 7 lb. but not over 28 lb.		...	...	2d.
Over 28 lb. but not over 56 lb.	...		...	4d.

These charges covered delivery within ½ mile of the tramways, but deliveries
were made up to a mile from tramway routes at an additional charge of 1d.
per package. Special terms were arranged with tradesmen sending regular
or large consignments, such as the daily distribution of newspapers from the
wholesale to retail newsagents. The question of conveying messages in the

form of letters arose, but the Postmaster General intervened and prohibited the practice as it contravened the Post Office Acts, and the Corporation had to give public notice that such packages could not be accepted. It was not unknown following this for letters to be put into a box and forwarded as a parcel! This revised Parcels Service was much more successful than its predecessor and receipts in the first year amounted to £460 against £21 in the last year of the old system. Total parcels carried was 74,394. A later development was the collection and delivery of books for the Central Branch of the Public Library and in 1916, after the introduction of road motor services in the Reading district by the British Automobile Traction Company and the Aldershot and District Traction Company, exchange arrangements were made with these companies for the conveyance of parcels throughout their areas.

On the 11th May, 1911, a tour of the entire tramway system was made by the Chairman of the Tramways and Highways Committees in a special car, accompanied by the Tramways manager, in order to inspect the state of the carriageways and compare the various methods of paving in use. They found the tracks in good order except for certain portions of Southampton Street where lava setts were used. The old question of centre poles was also considered, the removal of which it was estimated would cost about £3,000. As this work was entirely unnecessary from the point of view of the tramways it was decided to make application to the Road Board to see if that body would make a grant from its funds towards the project. The reply, however, stated that although the Board were of the view that the removal of the standards would be a very desirable improvement, it was not a work to which they were prepared to contribute. In spite of this refusal it was decided to proceed with the removal of the poles and an application was made to the Board of Trade for their sanction to the borrowing of the required sum, which in due course was granted. Concurrently with the foregoing a letter was received from the Board of Trade stating that it had been represented to them that in St. Mary's Butts near the junction of the Bath Road route, a less clearance than the required 15 in. existed between two or three of the centre poles and the top deck railings of passing cars. The Corporation's observations on the matter were called for, and in reply the manager stated that the tramway rails were laid and the poles erected in 1902 and 1903 when the tramways were constructed and that neither the poles nor the rails had been altered in any way since they were originally placed in position. Furthermore, it was politely pointed out, before the tramways were opened to the public, the Board's own inspector had closely examined every part of the system and passed it fit for operation. Subsequently in 1908 a second inspection had taken place and no exception had been taken to any part of the system on that occasion either. As a final shot, the Board of Trade was informed that the poles were to be removed anyway, and the whole matter ended as a case of " much ado about nothing." The last centre poles were in fact removed in 1913, being replaced partly by side poles with bracket arms or span wires and partly by suspension from rosettes attached to walls of adjacent buildings, for which privilege, the Corporation paid the property owners 1s. per annum.

The Coronation of H.M. King Edward VII took place on the 22nd June, 1911, the day being a record one for tramway traffic, 69,887 passengers being carried and £287 taken in fares. This amount exceeded by £40 the previous record of August Bank Holiday, 1903, when the system was but a week old. In connection with the Coronation celebrations the aged poor inhabitants of the Borough were given a dinner and were conveyed to and from the festivities by tramcar, free of charge.

View of original car shed 1903. Two additional roads were added to right of picture in 1904. The whole building was demolished in 1936.

A feature of tramway operation in Reading which calls for some mention was the special service run for football matches held at the Elm Park ground of the Reading Football Club. This ground was situated about $\frac{1}{4}$ mile from the Oxford Road route on which a greatly augmented service was provided between Broad Street and Kensington Road on the occasion of first team matches. To provide sufficient cars it was usually necessary to withdraw several vehicles from the " side roads " on which only skeleton services were maintained meanwhile, and divert them to the main line. Two conductors were carried on the special cars and it was an amazing but common sight to see 100 passengers on a four-wheeled car built to seat 48. The open top deck would be a jam-packed mass of humanity where one could at least breathe a little more freely than the inside passengers who were also emulating the proverbial sardines. The conductor's platform would have another dozen or so souls, while the rear buffer of the car would support five or six more hanging on outside the dash. The cars carried " Football Special " boards dropped into sockets in the buffer at either end, and after dropping their load returned empty for another. During the match, it was the practice in earlier years to park the specials on the single track between the Barracks and Oxford Road terminus, service cars turning short while the section was so obstructed, but with the growth of other vehicular traffic, this practice ceased and the cars were run back to depot. The crews of the football specials were issued with free tickets for the match, but of course they had to return to their cars before the game ended to be ready to carry the return crowds.

Several items of permanent way work were carried out in 1912, one being the removal of the cross-over in King's Road from Abbey Street to a more convenient position near Duke Street junction. Street improvements at the junction of London Road and London Street on the Erleigh Road route enabled the curves at this point to be relaid to a greater radius, and finally a considerable portion of the track in Southampton Street was repaved with granite setts in place of the lava setts previously used.

There were at this time 66 motormen and 60 conductors licensed, and commencing on 1st January, 1912, their conditions of employment were improved by the reduction of their weekly hours from 65 to 60 and the granting of one day's rest in seven. Mr. Binns, who had managed the undertaking since electrification, resigned in October, 1912, to take up an appointment abroad, and was succeeded by his chief assistant, Mr. G. F. Craven. The new second in command was Mr. J. M. Calder.

One of Mr. Binn's last acts as manager was to suggest that with a view to reducing the cost of electric power for the cars a battery and automatic reversible booster should be obtained, the former from the Tudor Accumulator Co., Ltd., of London and the latter from the Lancashire Dynamo and Motor Company of Trafford Park, Manchester. The proposal was agreed to by the Tramways Committee, and the equipment was purchased and put into service on 25th April, 1913. Formerly it had been necessary to run three out of the four generators to provide power for the cars, but now two only were sufficient to maintain the normal load and in addition to charge the battery through the booster Furthermore the battery was able to supply all the energy required for the first two hours every day (5.0 a.m.-7.0 a.m.) making a further saving in power costs. At the same time new chain grate stokers were fitted to the power station boilers.

About this time a suggestion was made that vestibule screens should be fitted to the cars, but the idea was turned down by the Committee, as in their opinion, " . . . it is unnecessary to provide screens on the tramcars for the protection of the motormen." There is no doubt that these men were " tough " when it came to facing the weather and one wonders how some of the present day bus drivers would feel about the absence of windscreens. Indeed, this recalls a story told to the writer by an inspector one recent winter. He, the inspector, had occasion to remonstrate with a bus driver for running late, the driver's excuse being that his windscreen wiper would not operate and the snow which was falling at the time obscured his view. He was horrified when the inspector (an old tram man) suggested running with the windscreen open. The inspector's final remarks on the subject cannot be put into print!

The new manager submitted a report in March, 1913, in which he proposed to speed up car services. The average speed of Reading cars, including time for stops and waiting at termini was stated to be only 7 m.p.h. compared with many other systems which exceeded 8 m.p.h. The existing and proposed services were as follows : —

	Existing service.	Proposed service.
Oxford Road/Wokingham Road	11 cars—5 mins.	10 cars—5 mins.
Erleigh/Caversham/Whitley	8 ,, 7½ ,,	8 ,, 7 ,,
Bath Road/London Road	4 ,, 10 ,,	3 ,, 12 ,,

The first two of the above proposals were carried out, but no alteration was made to the Bath Road-London Road service although it could well have been done, this being the leanest route in terms of revenue.

Early in 1913 the London and South Western Railway Company were promoting a Bill in Parliament, Clause 33 of which was to authorise the railway company to operate motor omnibuses and other road vehicles in connection with their railway system. In view of possible competition with the tramways, Reading Corporation lodged a petition against the Bill. In this action, the Corporation were not alone and in view of the large number of objections the railway company subsequently withdrew the clause from the Bill. The Reading Corporation themselves obtained an Act in 1913, authorising among other things the reconstruction of Caversham Bridge. The existing bridge was a very inadequate structure and the Urban District of Caversham having been brought within the Borough of Reading by the boundary extension of 1911, it was proposed to build a new bridge which would render possible an extension of the Caversham tram route over the river into Caversham proper.

There had been a number of suggestions regarding possible extension of the tramways, and in February, 1912, a sub-committee had been appointed " to consider and report upon the question of the desirableness of either extending the tramways or establishing a service of railless trolley cars or motor omnibuses in connection with the tramways undertaking." Since its appointment a number of meetings had been held and a visit of inspection made to the experimental Cedes Stoll railless car operating at West Ham, and at length a report was considered by the Council in September, 1913. The outcome of this was a decision to promote a Bill in Parliament which in due course became the Reading Corporation Act, 1914, and authorised among other things the following tramway extension.

TRAMWAY No. 1 (double line 3.68 chains in length) situated in Caversham Road, commencing at a point 9 ft. 6 in. north of the north side of Randolph Road and terminating at a point 140 ft. south of the south abutment of the *present* Caversham bridge.

TRAMWAY No. 2 (double line 1 furlong 4.5 chains in length) commencing at the termination of Tramway No. 1 and passing over the Caversham bridge *authorised by the Act of 1913* along Bridge Street and Church Road and terminating in the last-named road at a point 153 ft. east of St. Anne's Road.

Tramway No. 1 was merely a short line to connect the existing tramway to the new bridge. A proviso was also included " that so much of the said tramways as is proposed to be constructed in the part of any road the widening of which is authorised by the Act of 1913 shall not be constructed until such part has been widened." In point of fact it subsequently transpired that neither of the above lines was ever constructed, and thus Caversham, twice promised tramways never actually got them.

Section 8 of the Act was exercised, however, on several later occasions, and provided as follows : —

Notwithstanding anything contained in the Order of 1899, in the Act of 1900, or in this Act, the Corporation with the consent of the Board of Trade may : —

(a) make, maintain, alter or remove such cross-overs, passing places, sidings, junctions and other works in addition to those particularly specified in or authorised by the Acts relating to any of the tramways of the Corporation as they find necessary or convenient for the efficient working of those tramways or for forming junctions with other tramways or light railways or for providing access to any warehouses, stables or carriage houses or works of the Corporation.

(b) lay down double lines in lieu of single line or interlaced lines, or single line in lieu of double lines or interlaced lines, or interaced lines in lieu of double lines or single line on any of the tramways either when constructing the tramways or at any time thereafter.

(c) construct or take up and reconstruct any of their tramways in such a position in the road in which it is authorised to be constructed as they may think fit.

Powers were also included in the Act for the construction of certain trolley vehicle routes and the operation of motor omnibuses.

Turning of the points at the more important junctions in the centre of the town was done by point boys, but all others were moved by the motormen with point " irons." These were short iron bars about two feet in length with a chisel end, and it was thus necessary for cars to be brought to a stand when points required to be altered, the " harpooning "* of the point while the car was still moving not being possible with the short iron. With the increase of other vehicular traffic, it was found that the tramcars caused obstruction by stopping in the middle of a busy junction to alter points, particularly at the Cemetery Junction, so in November, 1913, an automatic electric point controller was installed here. In passing it may be mentioned that the short point irons were a kind of " motorman's friend " being pressed into service for many jobs other than the intended use, from re-railing a derailed car to quietening an obstreperous passenger !

Other permanent way work undertaken about this time was the relaying of some of the single-track sections in Wokingham Road and the renewal of a number of point tongues. A considerable amount of trolley wire was becoming due for renewal and in connection with this work the manager requested permission to purchase a motor tower wagon. The Committee, however, asked for further details of the requirements and the report on

---

* I am indebted to Mr. S. E. Harrison's book, " Tramways of Portsmouth," for this expression.

47

the subject contained passages which to the present-day reader are mildly amusing. The department possessed two tower wagons, one a light emergency wagon and the other a heavy vehicle suitable for pole planting, erection of bracket arms and heavy work generally. Both, of course, were horse-drawn, but owing to delay caused on several occasions by having to wait for a horse and driver, it had been fitted with a drawbar so that it could be towed out by a tramcar if a horse was not available. This method had two disadvantages, the first being that it was not always possible to run the towing car to the scene of the breakdown because the current might have to be cut off, and secondly having arrived at the spot, the wagon had to be moved out of the way every time a car passed, which operation required several men who might not be available. Furthermore a large part of the overhead work was carried out at night and frequently the tower wagon had only to be moved a few times during that period, for which a motor wagon would use very little petrol, but horse hire cost 1s. 6d. per hour! The average annual cost of horse hire was £60. In spite of these convincing arguments the question of obtaining a motor tower wagon was adjourned *sine die*.

A communication was received in May, 1914, from a tradesman who was desirous of coming to an agreement with the Corporation for placing on the cars small automatic machines for the supply of chocolate. The proposal was gone into very thoroughly but was not adopted.

In July the employees applied through their trade union for certain improvements in their working conditions, including the provision of windscreens on the cars. Mr. Craven announced that he was in communication with the makers of such screens and hoped to have a car so fitted at an early date, but the outbreak of war in August, 1914, put an end to this and several other developments, including the recently authorised tramway extension into Caversham.

To conclude this chapter on the pre-war years the following statistics for the financial year ended 31st March, 1914, give some idea of the position of the tramways. Passengers carried totalled 8,865,128 and the cars ran 941,303 miles with a gross revenue of £36,910. Working expenses were £20,564 and capital charges and income tax accounted for £11,926, leaving a net profit of £4,420. Of this sum £1,890 was carried to the Borough Fund for the relief of the rates and the balance of £2,530 was placed in the Tramways reserve fund which thereby amounted to £18,370. The manager submitted a long report showing the annual amount required to be set aside during the next twelve years to provide for track renewals and warned against appropriating the profits to aid the rates, but as so often was the case with municipal tramways, the warning went largely unheeded.

Plate I.

CHAPTER V.

THE WAR YEARS 1914-1919.

The effects of the outbreak of war were felt immediately by the Tramways Department. Within a month 40 men had left to join the forces and there were only just sufficient motormen remaining to maintain services. To ease the position slightly the London Road-Bath Road service was reduced to every 12 minutes instead of every 10, which saved one car and two crews daily. The Tramways Committee had recently inspected a number of different makes of motor omnibuses with a view to ordering vehicles for the services it was proposed to introduce following Royal Assent to the Corporation's Bill. They had chosen those manufactured by the Daimler Company, but the makers notified the Corporation that the War Department had taken all their available chassis and it was impossible to give even an approximate delivery date. Enquiries were also made of the R.E.T. Construction Company of Leeds regarding the possibility of obtaining trolley vehicles, but again delivery could not be promised for at least six months. In view of this the question of extensions was shelved until the cessation of hostilities.

As a result of the war, the schools of the town were reorganised, some becoming War Hospitals which necessitated the scholars being transferred to other schools often a considerable distance away. One case was that of Wilson Road School, the pupils of which had to attend another school in Wokingham Road on the opposite side of the town. To convey them each way twice daily, three bogie cars were required which added an additional strain to the depleted staff. By March, 1915, a total of 71 men had left the department for war service, representing 35% of the total staff at the outbreak of war. As a result of this, car mileage was cut by 16,500 miles compared with the previous year although electrical energy consumed was considerably more. This was attributed to the handling of the cars by unskilled motormen. In spite of this, however, the net profit for the year was a record at £4,648.

The electric tramways had now been in operation twelve years and some of the equipment on the cars was showing signs of wear. A large number of motor cases had been welded, armatures rewound and controllers repaired but it was fast becoming necessary to replace equipment by new material. As an experiment the 35 h.p. motors from bogie car No. 34 were fitted to one of the four-wheeled cars and tried on the hilly Whitley route with satisfactory results. It was therefore decided to order 12 new 40 h.p. motors from Dick, Kerr and Company, together with 12 type DB1 Form K3 controllers to refit all the bogie cars and release their motors for further use in the small cars. There was some delay in delivery of this equipment which eventually arrived in 1916.

An event of some significance was the proposal in 1915 by the British Automobile Traction Company to operate motor omnibuses in the Reading district. The Company wrote to the Tramways manager notifying their

50

intention and stating that their fares would in all cases be twopence in excess of the maximum tramway fare where the two services covered the same roads. The Corporation indicated that they did not object and instituted negotiations with the Company for the interchange of parcels traffic. The protective fares are in force on the Thames Valley Traction Company's buses to this day.

Parts of the repair shops at the Tramways Depot were given over to munition work which included the manufacture of over 50,000 eighteen-pounder shell billets, 125 electrical ground stations, 46 aerial targets and 20 spars for aircraft. In addition, three or four bays of the car sheds were taken over by the Royal Flying Corps for use as a training school for airmen, and were fitted up as an instructional bombing range. This necessitated a number of cars being left out in the open at night. The staff position became more and more acute and in December, 1915, it was found necessary to engage women as conductors, a number of whom were later trained as drivers. They worked a 48-hour week against the 60 hours of the men. Bell girls were also employed to assist the conductresses.

The Restricted Lighting Order came into force on 10th January, 1916, to conform with which it was necessary to paint all roof lights at the depot with green paint, and all exterior lights in the yard were dipped in blue lacquer. The interior lamps of the cars were also similarly dipped to half their depth and fitted with shades which were supplied free by the advertising contractors. The route lights for Caversham and Whitley (orange and white) were subdued by pasting white paper over the coloured discs, and the headlamps of the cars had buff paper pasted in the dash glasses. From enquiries made of other tramway undertakings it was found that few systems made use of the tramcar window blinds as in cases where blinds were drawn people desirous of boarding cars could not see if accommodation was available. Public street lighting was of course included in the restrictions and in view of this the car services were revised during the hours of darkness. In the interests of safety, speeds were reduced and an extra car put on the main line service in order to maintain the 5-minute headway. On the Erleigh Road-Caversham-Whitley triangle the frequency was reduced from 7 to $7\frac{1}{2}$ minutes, while the 12-minute London Road-Bath Road service was reduced to 15 minutes with the same number of cars.

It was fortunate that just before the outbreak of hostilities a quantity of permanent way material had been obtained, but owing to shortage of staff little work had been carried out in the way of track repairs. During the first half of 1916, some progress was made and the points of Palmer Park loop and at Culver Road on the main line and DeBeauvoir Road loop on the Erleigh Road route were renewed, but Mr. Craven warned the Tramways Committee that considerable arrears of track maintenance would have accrued and large sums would need to be spent as soon as possible after the war had ended. With this future work in view, several items of equipment had already been purchased, including a " Celerity " rail grinder, a welding plant and a Foden steam wagon.

The number of passengers carried in the year ended 31st March, 1917, for the first time exceeded 10,000,000 being 10,919,513, representing 124 journeys per head of the population of the town. During the year 133 special cars were provided free of charge for wounded soldiers from the local hospitals, incidentally resulting in the appearance of the bogie cars on the side roads. 150 men, 75% of the prewar staff, had now left to join the forces, of whom three had lost their lives.

51

Car services were suspended on Christmas Day, 1917, and ever since it has been the practice to suspend services on this day each year.

A communication was sent by the President of the Board of Trade to all tramway undertakings in April, 1918, requesting a 15% reduction of fuel consumed in generating electrical energy and a special sub-committee was set up in Reading to consider means by which the desired reduction could be achieved. In due course the following revision of car services was decided upon.

(a) Caversham-Whitley to operate every 6 minutes from 8.0 a.m. till 10.0 p.m.

(b) Bath Road-Erleigh Road to operate every 10 minutes from 8.0 a.m. till 10.0 p.m.

(c) London Road branch—Services to be suspended completely.

(d) Sunday services to commence an hour later (3.0 p.m.) on all routes.

It should be understood that the above referred to basic services only, workmen's services continued to be run as before. These alterations resulted in a saving of $8\frac{1}{2}\%$ in car mileage and further to assist the economy a number of stopping places were abolished while at the power station itself a quantity of coke was burnt with the coal. The complete withdrawal of the London Road service resulted in a considerable number of protests from residents in the neighbourhood so a skeleton service was introduced at peak hours only consisting of seven cars per day leaving London Road terminus for Broad Street at 8.2 a.m., 8,27 a.m., 12.27 p.m., 12.57 p.m., 1.22 p.m., 5.32 p.m. and 5.57 p.m. The reduced services operated until 6th April, 1919, and were successful in reducing coal consumption by 25%. Notwithstanding the fact that car mileage had been reduced by 87,675 miles during the year, a total of 15,979,829 passengers were carried, an increase of over two million on the previous year.

With the cessation of hostilities the department began the slow and difficult path back to normal. As the men returned from the forces the number of conductresses was gradually reduced until by the summer of 1919 they had all left. Operating costs were rising sharply and the following figures show the difference in prices paid for typical items of tramway equipment between 1914 and 1918:—

				1914	1918
Rails	...	...	...	£6 per ton	£17 10s. per ton
Setts	...	...	...	18s. ,, ,,	26s. ,, ,,
Cement	...	...	...	34s. ,, ,,	129s. ,, ,,
Trolley wire	...	...	...	£102 per mile	£189 per mile
Span wire	...	...	...	16s. 6d. per cwt.	49s. per cwt.
Gear wheels	...	...	...	£3 2s. each	£13 18s. each
Pinions	...	...	...	10s. ,,	£2 15s. 6d. each
Tyres	...	...	...	28s. ,,	£4 8s. 6d. ,,
Armature coils	...	...	...	£5 per set	£17 5s. per set
Trolley heads	...	...	...	26s. 3d. each	£2 16s. 3d. each
Trolley wheels	...	...	...	3s. 2d. ,,	4s. 3d. ,,
Oil	...	...	...	1s., per gall.	3s. per gall.
Tickets	...	..	...	3d. per 1,000.	1s. 3d. per 1,000.

Wages had risen similarly and the annual bill for this item was now £35,000 or approximately equal to the *total* revenue for 1914. The exceptional traffics carried during the war years had been achieved with cars loaded far beyond their normal capacity in a way that would not have been tolerated in time of peace, and this fact, coupled with the lack of maintenance, had left both track and cars in a seriously run-down condition. The writer has heard stories of motormen receiving electric shocks when they took hold of controller handles, due to perished insulation, although he is not prepared to vouch for the truth of this. The fact remained, however, that considerable sums would have to be spent to restore the tramways to a serviceable condition and a fare increase was inevitable.

In Reading the distances for which passengers could travel for 1d. exceeded even those given by many large and prosperous undertakings many of which were now charging a 1½d. minimum fare. It was not considered desirable to abolish the 1d. minimum in Reading so a new fare structure was evolved which, while retaining the 1d. fare, was·calculated to give the increased revenue desired. This was achieved by making nearly all the fare stages to and from the town centre (Broad Street-G.P.O. or West Street Junction) and requiring conductors to issue tickets to that point on inward journeys. After leaving the town centre it was then necessary to issue fresh tickets to every passenger on the car, so that cross-town passengers had to pay twice. The full fare table was as under : —

1d. stages (main line).

			Distance
Oxford Road	—Western Elms Avenue	...	0.85 mile
Western Elms Avenue	—Broad Street ...	...	0.80 ,,
Broad Street	—Fatherson Road ...	...	0.85 ,,
Fatherson Road	—Wokingham Road ...	...	0.90 ,,
Fatherson Road	—London Road ...	...	0.65 ,,

1½d. stages (main line).

Oxford Road	—Broad Street ...	...	1.65 miles
Broad Street	—Wokingham Road ...	...	1.75 ,,
Broad Street	—London Road ...	...	1.50 ,,

1d. stages (side roads).

Whitley	—West Street Junction	...	0.90 mile
West Street Junction	—Caversham	...	0.80 ,,
Bath Road	—Broad Street ...	...	0.80 ,,
Broad Street	—Royal Berks Hospital	...	0.80 ,,
R. Berks Hospital	—Erleigh Road ...	...	0.70 ,,

1½d. stages (side roads).

Erleigh Road	—Broad Street		1.50 miles

These new fares came into force on 13th January, 1919, but were subsequently slightly amended in that passengers were permitted to travel over any two consecutive 1d. stages for 1½d., e.g., Western Elms Avenue to Fatherson Road originally required the issue of two 1d. tickets, but became a 1½d. journey. The fare charged on the Football Specials between Broad Street and Kensington Road was increased to 3d. Workmen's fares in Reading were very low, the journey from Oxford Road to Wokingham Road for instance, at 1d. return gave a ride of 6.8 miles, and when a short while previously the Secretary of the Municipal Tramways Association had received this information from Reading in answer to a questionaire, he wrote asking for confirmation as he thought the distance far too great !

As a start to the renewal of equipment, 20 controllers (Type DB1 form K3) 36 circuit breakers and six sets of grid resistances were ordered from Dick Kerr & Company. The last item was for the bogie cars with which trouble was experienced every time there was a heavy or sudden rainfall. The fault lay with the surface water drains in Oxford Road which at the time were inadequate and unable to prevent flooding in the " dip " under the G.W.R. bridge. Water quickly accumulated at this point to a depth of a foot or more which was sufficient to submerge the resistances of the bogie cars, carried as they were below the car bodies between the bogie trucks. The new resistances were placed in the more conventional position below the stairs at one end of the car. Further purchases at this time were the long awaited motor tower wagon, another motor chassis to carry the welding plant and 400 tons of rails. A quantity of surplus tramway equipment was also purchased from Brighton Corporation, but exact details of this cannot be traced.

The post war trade recovery was reflected in a suggestion that advertisement posters should be placed in the car windows, but this was only agreed to on condition that the posters did not exceed 24 in. x 4 in. in size and were limited to one window on each side of a car. Another request came from the Reading Football Club for permission to stick fixture posters on the car buffers but this was not allowed.

Photo courtesy R. A. Hobbs.

Rebuilt Car No. 2. Note direct stairs, 4-window body and colour light route indicator box.

Pursuant to Section 8 of the Reading Corporation Act, 1914, it was proposed in November, 1919, to lay double line in place of the single in Oxford Road between Wilson Road and The Barracks and the Town Clerk served notice upon owners and occupiers of premises abutting on that part of the road to this effect. No objections were received to the proposal, and the Minister of Transport signified his consent on the understanding that no cars of greater width than 6 ft. 6 in. would be used thereon, and that the distance between the track centres would be 7 ft. 9 in. Relaying of the single track in Wokingham Road between Eastern Avenue and Palmer Park Avenue was also carried out at this time, but the carriageway here was not wide enough to permit doubling of the section. This was a pity, as with the exception of the line between The Barracks and Oxford Road terminus, it was the only single line on the main route, and was always an obstacle to the working of a service of greater frequency than 5 minutes. At such times as the pre-Christmas shopping period it was the practice to provide a 3-minute service on the main line which, being greater than the capacity of the Wokingham Road single track, always led to bunching and delays to the cars.

The long promised Corporation motor buses began running on the 6th December, 1919, on a route from Caversham Heights to Tilehurst, the original fleet consisting of three A.E.C. vehicles. Partly to avoid competition with the Oxford Road trams, these buses ran via Tilehurst Road and Waverley Road, making connection with the trams at Oxford Road terminus. The introduction of the buses was the last major development during Mr. Craven's regime as General Manager as he resigned a month later to take up a position with a local firm of engineers. He returned to municipal transport later in his career, however, becoming manager of the Halifax Corporation undertaking, from which position he retired in 1947, being honoured the same year with the O.B.E. for outstanding services to passenger transport. Mr. Craven was succeeded at Reading by his former chief assistant, Mr. James McLennan Calder, who incidentally had just returned from a period " on loan " to Southampton Corporation Tramways. The change of managership forms a convenient point at which to conclude this chapter.

CHAPTER VI.

REHABILITATION—1920-1929.

Reading Corporation Tramways and Motors, to give the department its new full name, was going through an extremely difficult period of its career when Mr. Calder took over the reins. "Jimmy" Calder, as he was affectionately known throughout the municipal departments had been on the staff of the tramways undertaking since the early days of electric traction and he had worked through the various positions in the engineering department so was well acquainted with the problems facing him. A member of a race of engineers, the Scots, he combined his engineering experience with a shrewd business mind, and had a likeable sense of humour. The author recalls hearing him talking about his childhood and saying, " . . . the only thing I knew about tramways was how to get a free ride by hanging on the back of a Glasgow horse tram!"

It will probably be advantageous in this chapter to forsake the strict chronological order of events and to record developments separately under three headings, (a) Services and Fares, (b) Track and (c) Cars.

Services and Fares.

For the first two years of Mr. Calder's managership the department faced a deficit; £4,331 in 1920 and £14,023 in 1921. These were in fact the only two years in which the tramways were "in the red," indeed for many years they enabled the department as a whole to show a profit in spite of heavy losses on the omnibus side. In July, 1920, the new manager reported, "the financial position of the department is such that every effort should be made to improve it at the earliest opportunity. With a view to reducing the car mileage of the tramway service and consequently the running expenses of the department, I suggest that the services now running be altered. On the main line the cars running could well be reduced from 14 to 12, which means an economy of 38,354 miles per annum. On the side roads, by running cars from Whitley to Caversham and from Bath Road to Erleigh Road a saving of a further 33,018 miles per annum could be effected, giving a total reduction of 71,372 miles per annum." London Road was to be provided with a service to and from Broad Street only. The following table sets out the alterations in detail.

Existing routes and annual mileages.

Oxford Road—Wokingham Road	...	...	504,806
Erleigh Road—Caversham—Whitley	...	...	265,492
Bath Road—London Road	...	...	...	101,940
Specials	...	...	15,808
All routes Sundays	...	...	...	86,474

974,520

56

Proposed routes ond annual mileages.

Oxford Road—Wokingham Road	... ...	466,452
Caversham—Whitley	... ...	177,026
Erleigh Road—Bath Road	... ...	119,952
London Road—Broad Street	... ...	53,244
Sundays	... ...	86,474
		903,148

Existing total	974,520	
Proposed total	903,148	
Saving ...	71,372	

The proposed new services were put into operation and continued until December, 1920, when further modifications resulted in the restoration of the Erleigh Road-Caversham-Whitley triangle and a reduced Bath Road-London Road service (20 minutes). On the main line, yet another car was taken off leaving 11 cars. At one period an attempt was made to work a 20-minute service on Sundays between London Road and Broad Street with only one car, but this was more than the human frame could stand as it was all of a 10-minute journey each way, leaving no terminus standing time at all. No crews could be expected to do 8 hours of this non-stop, so a second car was put on and a 15-minute service provided.

To add to the troubles of the tramways department, a strike occurred in the coal mining industry in April, 1921, and it was again necessary to conserve fuel supplies. To achieve this, the unfortunate Bath Road-London Road service suffered another period of complete suspension and *all* tram services were withdrawn on Sundays. In place of the Sunday trams, three of the recently acquired motor omnibuses were used to provide a 15-minute service on the main line tram route . . . at double tram fares ! Normal services were restored on 10th July, 1921.

The recently passed Tramways (Temporary Increase of Charges) Act, 1920, did not provide the department with any means of adding to its revenue by way of increased fares, as the powers granted by the original Reading Tramways Order of 1878 were not yet fully exercised. To take advantage of these powers a minimum fare of 2d. could be charged, and even then it would be necessary to have shown a loss at this higher fare before an application could be made under the 1920 Act. As it was very undesirable to increase the minimum fare to 2d. if it could be avoided, the following new fare structure was introduced.

Stages—

Broad Street (G.P.O.)			
or West Street	—Western Elms Avenue ...	1,496	yards
	—Bath Road	1,362	,,
	—Whitley	1,513	,,
	—Redlands Road	1,649	,,
	—Fatherson Road	1,515	,,
	—Caversham	1,355	,,
Western Elms Avenue	—Oxford Road	1,390	,,
Redlands Road	—Erleigh Road	1,068	,,
Fatherson Road	—Wokingham Road ...	1,584	,,
	—London Road	1,101	,,

An "overlap stage" was later introduced between Watlington Street and Cemetery Junction. Charges for the above were 1st stage 1½d.; 2nd stage 2d.; 3rd and 4th stages 3d. Mention of Cemetery Junction brings to mind one tram conductor who had the reputation of being rather a wag. It was his habit on arriving at Cemetery Junction to call out, "Marble Arch—change for the underground!" To appreciate this fully, the reader should understand that the entrance to Reading Cemetery is in the form of a rather imposing archway.

For some considerable time dogs had not been allowed upon the tram-cars, but from October, 1921, this regulation was rescinded and canine friends could accompany passengers, although suffering the indignity of being issued with a "parcel" ticket!

The Summer timetable introduced on 2nd April, 1922, contained a new "Sundays only" service from London Road to Caversham. This was immediately popular as it provided a through service from the east end of the town to the Thames-side Promenade, a favourite local pleasure resort. This service remained a regular feature of the summer services until the abandonment of the Caversham route. Details of the new Sunday services were as under :—

Commencing at 2.0 p.m.—

Oxford Road	-Wokingham Road ...	12 cars—	5-minute service.		
Caversham	Whitley	6 „	— 6	„	,,
London Road	Caversham ...	2 „	—20	„	,,
Bath Road	Erleigh Road ...	3 „	—15	„	,,

The fare table for the Caversham-London Road route was as follows :—

1½d. stages—
Broad Street   —Caversham.
Fatherson Road—West Street Junction.
London Road   —Fatherson Road.

2d. stages—
London Road   —West Street Junction.
Fatherson Road—Caversham.

3d. stage—
London Road   —Caversham.

The financial year ended 31st March, 1922, restored the balance to the "right side" once more with a net profit of £2,988. Less satisfactory was the fact that the Reserve Fund now contained only £31! In view of this, the usual raiding of profits to relieve the rates did not occur, and the whole profit was placed in reserve. The Tramways Committee were doubtless very pleased with the year's results and they took the rather unusual step of officially recording in their minutes the following resolution—"That the Committee do record their appreciation of the general manager and engineer's management of the tramway undertaking."

A further sign that the department was beginning to get back "on its feet" was the reintroduction of 1d. fares as from 1st July, 1923, when the following fare list came into force.

1d. stages (main line).
Oxford Road   —Elm Park Road.
Elm Park Road   —Russell Street.
Russell Street   —Duke Street Junction.
West Street Junction —Watlington Street.
Watlington Street   —Cemetery Junction.
Cemetery Junction   —Wokingham Road.

$1\frac{1}{2}d.$ *stages* (*main line*).

Oxford Road	—Western Elms Avenue.
Western Elms Avenue	—Duke Street Junction.
West Street Junction	—Fatherson Road.
Fatherson Road	—Wokingham Road.

$2d.$ *stages* (*main line*).

Oxford Road	—Broad Street (G.P.O.).
Western Elms Avenue	—Fatherson Road.
West Street Junction	—Wokingham Road.

$3d.$ *stage* (*main line*).

Oxford Road	—Wokingham Road.

$1d.$ *stages* (*side roads*).

Caversham	—Tudor Road.
Tudor Road	—Mill Lane.
Mill Lane	—Whitley.
Tudor Road	—Duke Street.
Erleigh Road	—Redlands Road.
Redlands Road	—West Street Junction.
Duke Street Junction	—Mill Lane.
London Road	—Fatherson Road.
West Street Junction	—Bath Road.

$1\frac{1}{2}d.$ *stages* (*side roads*).

Caversham	—Mill Lane.
Tudor Road	—Whitley.
Erleigh Road	—Duke Street Junction.
Caversham	—Duke Street Junction.
Whitley	—Duke Street Junction.
Bath Road	—Duke Street Junction.
London Road	—Watlington Street.

$2d.$ *stages* (*side roads*).

Caversham	—Whitley.
Caversham	—Redlands Road.
Caversham	—Fatherson Road.
Erleigh Road	—West Street Junction.
Redlands Road	—Whitley.
London Road	—West Street Junction.
Fatherson Road	—Bath Road.
Redlands Road.	—Bath Road.

$3d.$ *stages* (*side roads*).

Caversham	—Erleigh Road.
Erleigh Road	—Whitley.
Bath Road	—London Road.
Caversham	—London Road.
Bath Road	—Erleigh Road.

The foregoing fare structure remained in force substantially unaltered for the remainder of the life of the tramways, the only alterations being a few slight adjustments in the $1\frac{1}{2}d.$ and 2d. stages which were to the advantage of passengers.

This stabilising of fares is perhaps an opportune point at which to record details of the tickets in use which, like the fares, remained little altered

59

hereafter. The Punch and Ticket Company of London supplied all tickets required, which were as follows:—

1d. Ordinary (Red).

1½d. ,, (Blue).

2d. ,, (White).

3d. ,, (Green).

2d. Workmen's Return (Buff).

— Workmen's Exchange (Lilac with red " W " overprint).

— Education Exchange (Yellow with red " EE " overprint).

1d. Exchange (Yellow with " E1d " overprint in red).

1½d. ,, (Buff ,, " E1½d." ,, ,, ,,).

2d. ,, (Salmon ,, " E2d." ,, ,, ,,).

1d. Parcel Ticket (White with vertical blue stripe and red overprint " Parcel 1d.").

In addition to the above, there were various forms of prepaid discount tickets, scholars' tickets and special tickets for postmen under the contract with the G.P.O. The colours and forms mentioned above were those in general use, although in the early days there had been considerable variation from time to time. Originally the value of a ticket was shown by a large overprint, but the final style showed the value as part of the printed text of the ticket. All tickets except the Workmen's Return were geographical. with names of the stages printed in full, and were punched against the stage to which a passenger was entitled to travel. The workmen's ticket had odd numbers 1 to 31 down the left hand side and even numbers 2 to 30 on the right. These numbers represented date of issue and tickets were punched accordingly. The month of issue was not shown and consequently there was a certain amount of misuse of these tickets by persons who for any reason failed to make the return journey on the day of issue and held the ticket until the same date next month. It was suggested that the colours of workmen's tickets should be varied from day to day, to overcome this misuse, but the authorities did not consider it sufficiently serious to warrant the expense.

Prepaid discount tickets were sold for all values in use, in books of 12 tickets for the price of 10, but were not accepted in payment of workmen's. children's half fares or scholars' fares. The discount tickets were in two halves, one of which was retained by the conductor, the other returned to the passenger together with an exchange ticket.

One or two curious errors occurred from time to time in the printing of the tickets, one being the transposing of the initials of the undertaking. so that they appeared as " R.T.C." instead of " R.C.T.", but these should not be mistaken for tickets of the Reading Tramways Company. Another rather amusing mistake occurred in a batch of Workmen's Exchange tickets and Education Exchange tickets, when the printers transposed the texts and overprints so that one had Workmen's Exchanges bearing the information that they were " Issued in exchange for Education ticket " and vice versa.

Although not directly concerned with this account of the tramways, it is of interest to note that workmen's fares were introduced on the Corporation motor buses in July, 1924, the workmen's buses on the Tilehurst route operating a shuttle service between Tilehurst and Oxford Road tram ter-

Plate II.

minus only, where passengers had to change to a tramcar for the rest of the journey to town. There was no through booking, two separate fares being paid.

Throughout their history Reading Corporation Tramways enjoyed good relations between management and staff, the only blot on the record being the General Strike of 1926, this of course being national and not merely local. Cars ceased running on Tuesday, 4th May and normal working was not resumed until Wednesday, 12th. In the meantime, skeleton services were provided by about nine of the staff who remained at work, supplemented by Mr. Calder himself who carried out a motorman's duty. A police officer rode on the driver's platform of all cars operating and apart from a few broken windows nothing untoward occurred. During the strike cars carried a large poster in the windows, " Fare 2d., Broad Street to Terminus—Either way " and ran more or less as required, there being no timetable. When the strike ended about half-a-dozen men attempted to prevent cars leaving the depot and fell into the hands of the police. With the exception of these men, all employees were re-engaged.

Mention should be made of the administrative system employed in operating the traffic department of the undertaking. The three services were lettered " A " (main line), " B " (Bath Road-London Road) and " C " (Erleigh Road-Caversham-Whitley) although no indication was made on the cars of the route letters. The eleven basic car duties on the main line were lettered A, B, C, etc., to K; the three cars on route " B " were known as BA, BB and BC, while the eight cars employed on service " C " were CA, CB, CC and so on to CH. It will be seen then that the first letter of the combination refers to the route and the second letter to the car, although in the case of the main line, the initial " A " was always omitted. Cars were arranged as far as possible to follow each other in service in alphabetical order, although this was not a hard and fast rule. The crew duties took the letter of their respective cars in the case of the " early " turn men, thus " BC " car was " BC " crew duty, but the " late " turn men who relieved them were duty " BC2."

The men themselves worked through the duties in alphabetical order, viz., A, A2, B, B2, C, C2 and so on, although the sequence was broken periodically by a " relief week " when a crew would be on a different duty each day, covering men who were on their rest day.

Commencing about July, 1926, a new motor bus service was introduced between Oxford Road tram terminus and the Roebuck Hotel, Oxford Road, Tilehurst. This shuttle service ran until 11th April, 1927, after which date the buses ran right through to Reading stations via Grovelands Road and Waverley Road, thus avoiding direct competition with the trams. On the 21st March, 1928, this omnibus service was again revised and thereafter was routed along Oxford Road over the tram route, and extended from the stations to Workingham Road (Three Tuns Inn) via Redlands Road, Addington Road and Crescent Road. On the Oxford Road section protective fares were in force to avoid direct competition with the trams, although tha bus service was only every 20 minutes against the $4\frac{1}{2}$-5-minute service of the trams. The eastern half of the bus route served the same district as the Erleigh Road tram service, but direct competition was again avoided by the use of back streets by the buses.

In March, 1929, the general manager announced that at long last the department had been able to produce a time-table booklet for issue to the public, and this gave the following tramcar services : —

Workmen's Car services.

Oxford Road to Wokingham Road	...	5.30	7.00	7.33
		5.54	7.06	7.34
		6.18	7.18	7.36
		6.30	7.25	7.39
		6.42	7.28	7.41
		6.54	7.30	7.42
Wokingham Road to Oxford Road	...	5.30	6.42	7.25
		5.54	6.54	7.30
		6.18	7.06	7.35
		6.30	7.18	7.38
		—	—	7.42
London Road to Broad Street		7.15	—	—
		7.40	—	—
Whitley to Caversham		5.45	6.45	7.15
		6.15	7.00	7.30
		—	—	7.45
Caversham to Whitley		6.00	7.00	7.30
		6.30	7.15	7.45
Erleigh Road to Broad Street		7.45	—	—

No workmen's service was provided on the Bath Road route.

Ordinary Car services.

Cars leave			Weekdays Every	Weekdays First	Weekdays Last	Sundays Every	Sundays First	Sundays Last
Oxford Rd.	for	Wok'ham Rd.	5 min.	7.47	10.49	5 min.	2.00	10.15
,,	,,	Depot	,,	—	11.13	,,	—	10.42
Wok'ham Rd.	,,	Oxford Rd.	,,	7.47	10.47	,,	2.00	10.15
,,	,,	Depot	,,	—	11.15	,,	—	10.42
Whitley	,,	Caversham	15 min.	7.53	10.53	6 min.	2.00	10.20
,,	,,	Depot	,,	—	11.08	,,	—	10.35
,,	,,	Erleigh Rd.	,,	8.00	10.45	—	—	—
Caversham	,,	Whitley	,,	7.45	10.45	6 min.	2.00	10.20
,,	,,	Depot	,,	—	11.07	,,	—	10.35
,,	,,	Erleigh Rd.	,,	7.53	10.52	—	—	—
Erleigh Rd.	,,	Whitley	,,	7.46	10.45	—	—	—
,,	,,	Caversham	,,	7.53	10.38	—	—	—
,,	,,	Depot	,,	—	11.15	—	—	—
Bath Rd.	,,	London Rd.	20 min.	8.15	9.55	—	—	—
London Rd.	,,	Bath Rd.	,,	7.55	9.35	—	—	—
,,	,,	Depot	,,	—	10.24	—	—	—
Erleigh Rd.	,,	Broad St.	—	—	—	15 min.	2.00	10.15
Broad St.	,,	Erleigh Rd.	—	—	—	,,	1.45	10.30
Erleigh Rd.	,,	Depot	—	—	—	,,	—	10.45

TRACK.

A start was made in 1920 in connection with track renewals by ordering from Hadfields, Ltd., of Sheffield the special work required for the four junctions on the system, and a contract was signed with Messrs. Scholey & Company of Westminster for the hardening of two miles of track by the " Sandberg-Insitu " process as a temporary measure to preserve the track until complete relaying could be undertaken. Impressions and measurements of rail sections were taken from time to time at different points on the system to check the wear of rails, and in October, 1923, it was decided to relay the section between Factory Bridge and Eldon Road on the main line at a cost of £3,260. In the December following, approval was given for the expenditure of a further £500 for similar work in Duke Street on the Erleigh Road line. In February, 1924, the permanent way question was gone into thoroughly and the following schedule prepared for renewals.

Job No.	Section	Date
1	Palmer Park Loop	1924
2	West Street Junction	1924
3	Broad Street	1924
4	Duke Street Junction	1925
5	Cemetery Junction—Eldon Road	1925
6	Wilson Road—Reading West Station ...	1926
7	Reading West Station—West Street ...	1927
8	Greyfriars Curve	1928
9	Bulmershe Road Loop	1928
10	Vastern Road Curve	1928
11	Watlington Street—Duke Street	1929

(It will be noted from the following pages that this programme was not carried out in the order shown above).

The total cost of the relaying programme was estimated to be £70,000 and an application was made to the Ministry of Transport for sanction to the borrowing of this sum. After one or two minor hitches due to the Ministry suggesting various modifications to the layout with which the Corporation were not in agreement, the matter was settled with the following conditions.

(a) Work No. 2 (West Street Junction): That a minimum clearance of 15 in. be provided between the sides of cars and the kerb on the south-east curve between Broad Street and St. Mary's Butts, the kerb being set back if necessary.

(b) Work No. 5 (Cemetery—Eldon Road): That the southern of the two tracks be moved northward when reconstruction takes place in order to provide a clearance of 10 ft. between the southern kerb and the tramway rail.

(c) Work No. 11 (Watlington Street—Duke Street): That the tramway tracks on Crown Bridge, which it is understood is to be rebuilt, be closed together to the usual interval of 7 ft. 9 in. between centres, the cable duct being altered in position if necessary.

The first instalment of the loan amounting to some £12,000 was obtained in 1925 to cover items Nos. 2, 3 and 8 of the programme, the rails being supplied by Bolckow, Vaughan & Company, Ltd., of Middlesbrough, and the creosoted wood blocks by the Improved Wood Pavement Co., Ltd., of Blackfriars, London. A piece of vacant land in Cheapside was rented for use as a dump and depot for the materials. Work began in May, 1925, in Broad Street, and was completed before the scheduled time without a hitch, making it possible to commence work on the complicated West Street Junction a week earlier than had been anticipated. Operations on this site commenced at 11.30 p.m. on Saturday, 20th June, 1925, immediately the last car of the day had passed. Special arrangements had to be made for all types of traffic, as the junction, the busiest in Reading, was closed completely, all ordinary vehicular traffic being diverted. Tramcar services were cut and worked to and from this point, cars on the sections remote from the depot had of course to remain out at night. Within six days, main line tram services were restored over the new track and efforts were then turned to the connecting curves from Broad Street to West Street and St. Mary's Butts, which were complicated by the existence of a network of water and gas mains, sewers, electric cables, etc. Day and night shifts were worked and the entire job was completed in three weeks.

The third item (No. 8) was the reverse curves in Friar Street on the Caversham route, which was carried out without any special difficulties, but it is of interest to record that provision was made for these curves to be water lubricated.

The next sections to be dealt with were items Nos. 4, 5 and 10 which were scheduled for the year ending 31st March, 1927, at a cost of £12,666. This work was delayed somewhat by the General Strike of May, 1926, but Duke Street Junction was dealt with in August. The rails for this year's programme were supplied by the Equipment and Engineering Co., Ltd., of Strand, London. On the longer lengths of double line, one track was dealt with at a time, temporary cross-overs being provided where necessary to enable services to be maintained on the other track, working being by means of a " staff " as in railway practice.

An event of some interest to the tramways was the opening in May, 1926, of the new Caversham Bridge. This bridge which had been authorised in 1913 was, it will be remembered, intended to carry tramway tracks into Caversham. The powers granted by the 1914 Act for this extension had expired, however, and as the Corporation was now operating motor omnibuses over the bridge, there was no likelihood of any new tramway powers being obtained. Road widening works on the Reading side of the bridge necessitated the removal of the tram tracks at the Caversham terminus to a more convenient position, and accordingly they were diverted into the approach road to the Thames-side Promenade, enabling trams to draw up alongside the kerb, well off the main Caversham Road. This trackwork was carried out under Section 8 of the Reading Corporation Act, 1914, and had no connection with the track relaying programme, being paid for out of Reserve Fund.

Following the re-siting of the terminus, cars waiting there could not be seen by intending passengers approaching over the bridge, so a signal lamp was placed on an adjacent standard, facing towards Caversham, being lit automatically as each car arrived and extinguished as it left the terminus. A similar arrangement was installed on the London Road branch to indicate to anyone in Cholmeley Road that a car was at the terminus.

About this time, the General Manager was instructed to prepare a report on the question of laying a tramway siding in Wantage Road for the use of Football Special cars. This would have been a very useful project, but probably due to the industrial troubles at the time, which were already making it difficult to obtain the rails for the relaying programme, the idea was not proceeded with.

The third instalment of the loan for track renewals, amounting to £21,700 was obtained for work to be carried out in the year ending March, 1928, on items Nos. 7 and 11. These were in Oxford Road between the G.W.R. bridge and West Street and in King's Road from Watlington Street to Duke Street.

Traffic congestion was being experienced at the Oxford Road terminus, where the cars stood in the middle of the busy main road at its junction with Grovelands Road, and to remedy this a proposal was made for the modification of the track layout. Three schemes were considered (1) extension of the track into Grovelands Road, (2) extension along Oxford Road to a siding on the south side of that road and (3) extension into Craig Avenue, a private Road. The Craig Avenue scheme was decided upon and the necessary notices served on " owners and occupiers of houses, shops or warehouses abutting upon those portions of road where the rail was intended to be laid in such a manner that a space less than 9 ft. in. would intervene between such rail and the outside of the footpath." (Section 8—1914 Act). Unfortunately opposition to the scheme arose from the landowners and much correspondence passed. Eventually the objectors offered to waive their objections subject to certain conditions, namely : —

(a) That the Corporation indemnified the owners against any private street improvement charges.
(b) That there should be no extension of the tramway beyond the point shown on the plan.
(c) That if at any time the tramway was extended along Oxford Road, the Craig Avenue terminus would be abandoned.
(d) That the Corporation pay all legal and surveyor's charges in the matter.

In view of all the circumstances, the proposal to lay a tramway siding in Craig Avenue was not proceeded with, but this was not the end of the matter, as will be seen anon.

Concurrently with the unsuccessful Oxford Road scheme, a proposal was received with regard to the Wokingham Road terminus. The owner of the land lying in the fork of Wokingham Road and St. Peter's Road had applied to the Corporation for permission to erect thereon a building to be used as tea rooms, and in consideration of being granted such permission

View showing Wokingham Road terminus as resited in reservation.
Compare this photograph taken about 1938 with that on page 42.

was prepared to relinquish free of charge, a part of the plot for street improvements. This offer was accepted, enabling the tram track to be extended about 25 yards into what was virtually a reserved track terminus. Cars now stood well off the main Wokingham Road and passengers could board or alight in safety. The tea rooms became known as the " Terminus Cafe," and are still so named at the present time, although there is no longer a terminus at this point.

The relaying of the two loops in Wokingham Road, items Nos. 1 and 9 of the programme were presumably only small jobs and were carried out without the need to raise a loan for the purpose. This left only item No. 6, the section in Oxford Road between Wilson Road and the railway bridge, for which the fourth and final instalment of the loan was obtained, amounting to £15,000. The work was carried out during the summer of 1928 and in the process, the cross-over at Kensington Road, used by the Football Specials was resited at Wantage Road, rendering the destination indicator for " Kensington Road " redundant. " Wantage Road " was added to all blinds except those on cars Nos. 7 and 16 which for some reason (probably oversight) retained the old indication. It will be noted incidentally that the entire relaying programme had been carried out for considerably less cost than was at first estimated.

In January, 1928, it was decided to equip most of the single-track sections with automatic signals and an order for ten sets of apparatus was placed with The Equipment and Engineering Co., Ltd. When delivered, the signals were erected on the following sections : —

Main line—Wokingham Road.	Cemetery Junction/Bulmershe Road.
	Bulmershe Road/Palmer Park Loop.
	Palmer Park Loop/Culver Road.
Oxford Road.	Barracks/Oxford Road terminus.
Erleigh Road section.	Duke Street/Mill Lane.
	Kendrick Road/London Street (top).
	Kendrick Road/Albion Place.
	Albion Place/Craven Road.
	Craven Road/Alexandra Road.
	Alexandra Road/DeBeauvoir Road.

The equipment consisted of two-aspect coloured light signals housed in boxes attached to the overhead standards and operated by the passage of the car trolleys through " skates " on the overhead. A car on striking a skate set up a green light for itself and a red light at the opposite end of the section. On leaving the far end of the single line, contact with a second skate extinguished the lights.

At the very time when the signals would be thought to be of the greatest use, i.e., in foggy weather, drivers were instructed to ignore them and work to a system of pre-arranged passing places. A duplicated sheet was issued to all drivers setting out these passing places, extracts from which are given below.

PASSING PLACES IN FOGGY WEATHER.

Workmen's Traffic		Passing Place
5.30 a.m.-7.00 a.m.	(Oxford Road)	Barracks.
5.30 a.m.-7.18 a.m.	(Wokingham Road)	Cemetery Junction.
From 7.00 a.m.	(Oxford Road)	Barracks.
From 7.18 a..m.	(Wokingham Road)	Palmer Park Loop and Cemetery Junction.

Main line passing places—
4-minute service

    Cemetery Junction.
    Bumershe Road.
    Culver Road.

5-minute service

    Cemetery Junction.
    Palmer Park Loop.

Caversham—Whitley—
7½-minute service

    Mount Street.

NOTE.—All specials to run to Barracks only.

Wokingham Road and Culver Road specials to run to London Road. The cross over in Southampton Street MUST NOT BE USED in foggy weather.

Special attention must be given when midday and evening specials are running.

Tramway signal lamps to be ignored in foggy weather.

When the track between Cemetery Junction and Eldon Road was relaid in 1926, the actual junction was found still to have some useful life and consequently it had been left untouched. By June, 1929, however, it was found necessary to complete the relaying of the junction, and the work was therefore carried out, being the last relaying operation as such to be done on the Reading tramways. A number of other sections were subsequently relaid, but as part of road widening works and not as renewals. A new point controller was provided at Cemetery Junction concurrently with the relaying, and a further five such machines were purchased and installed at West Street and Duke Street junctions.

Photo Courtesy H. B. Priestley.

A group of vestibuled cars. The " Under Repair " board on No. 15, and the pronounced " list " of this car probably indicates a broken axle.

The process of rebuilding the cars was spread over about 10 years, 1920-1929. As each car became earmarked for attention it was not immediately withdrawn from traffic, but continued in service painted in a flat grey with white numerals and the initials " R.C.T." only on the rocker panels. New bodies were being constructed at Mill Lane depot meanwhile, and as each new body was ready one of the grey cars would be brought in and the body exchanged for a new one. In all probability there were some spare trucks (possibly from the ex-Brighton equipment) as about this time four 21E " wide wing " trucks made their appearance under cars Nos. 5, 6, 8 and 14, which presumably released an equal number of old trucks for reconditioning or scrap. A mystery surrounded the truck of No. 13, the main side frames of which bore evidence of having been welded exactly midway between the axle box guides, arousing suspicions of its having had a section cut out to shorten the wheelbase. This truck may have been a second hand one suitably adapted to Reading's requirements. There was also a truck with Brill swing axle fittings to the axle-boxes which appeared under various cars, being last noted on No. 17 about 1928-29 after which it disappeared, and this car had the normal Brill 21E truck.

All but one of the four-wheeled cars were rebuilt, the exception being No. 10 which will be mentioned later. The new cars had four window bodies and direct $\frac{1}{4}$-turn stairs in place of the reversed pattern previously used. Nos. 4, 5, 7 and 11 differed from the remainder in that they had rounded corners to the bulkhead door frames, all other cars having rectangular doors. These four cars (and No. 10) retained their old type DB1 form B controllers whereas all the other cars were fitted with new form K3 controllers. This is probably an indication of the order of rebuilding, as the rounded doors were a feature of the original bodies which may have been retained in the earlier rebuilds. No record exists of the actual rebuilding dates of individual cars, but Nos. 2, 13 and 17 were among the earlier conversions, while the last to be dealt with in the pre-vestibule period was No. 6, after which cars were rebuilt and vestibuled as one operation, details of which appear later in this chapter.

Owing to the removal of the reversed stairs, the route indicator light was now carried in a small wooden box fixed to the canopy and above the driver's head. These boxes were in effect small cupboards, and in addition to the lamp and coloured discs, they were often used to store anything from the conductor's copper-bags to the driver's dinner. Between the two canopy stancions a horizontal rail was fitted at about driver's eye level which seemed to fulfil no other purpose than impede his vision. A slight re-arrangement of the top deck seats was necessary by reason of the altered position of the stairs and there was now a curved seat for three on each canopy. Interior seating remained longitudinal, but Nos. 9 and 14 were upholstered in leather and Nos. 1, 8, 19, 20, 25 and 30 received cushioned seats in grey moquette, all the remaining cars retaining wooden seating. No. 1 and bogie car No. 36 were fitted with air push-bells, but all others had the cord operated variety. On rebuilding, small wooden oval-shaped number plates were fitted over the doors inside the passenger saloons bearing, in addition to the car number, the words " Rebuilt at Mill Lane Depot." No. 30 was fitted with a pair of Metropolitan Vickers controllers about this time.

In February, 1925, it was decided as an experiment to fit a car with vestibule ends, and No. 19 appeared in due course so equipped. After running thus through the following winter to obtain the motormen's reactions to the alteration it was decided to extend the idea, and Nos. 1, 9, 25 and 30 were also given vestibules on rebuilding, while Nos. 7, 8, 11, 15 16, 17, 20 and 29 which were already rebuilt had vestibules added, making a total of thirteen cars so fitted. No. 19, the first one, had a somewhat lighter type of framework to the vestibules than was fitted to the others. One would hardly have thought there would have been any doubt as to the men's views on the " glasshouses " as the vestibuled cars became known, but one man was said to complain that they were draughty! It is not recorded how he described the open cars.

Another minor event about this time was the fitting of one car, believed to be No. 21 with solid disc wheels in place of the usual spoked variety. The main result was a host of complaints about the noise the car made, its metallic " clang, clang " at each joint being audible long before it appeared. The offending wheels were therefore soon removed.

Consideration was given in May, 1925, to the fitting of Royal Mail letter boxes on the cars, and the matter was discussed with the Head Postmaster of Reading, but the suggestion was not entertained.

Mention should be made of the decorated cars which made their appearance from time to time. The first recorded one was for the Victory celebrations of 1919, while in September, 1923, the Mayor of Reading opened a fund for the relief of distress through unemployment, for which a car, believed to have been No. 1, was decorated and fitted each end with a large figure of a black cat, the eyes of which rolled round and round, operated by a pendulum device governed by the swaying of the car. Special 1d. tickets were on sale by the conductors to raise funds for the cause. These tickets were white with two red vertical lines and bore the words, " Received with thanks one penny, for the Mayor's Unemployment Relief Fund." Another car was illuminated with hundreds of bulbs for " Health Week," 1924.

As mentioned earlier, the only four-wheeled car which was not rebuilt was No. 10. On this car, the original three window body was retained, but the new pattern direct stairs were fitted. The old type DB1 form B controllers were not replaced and, for a considerable time, the truck boasted odd axle boxes, one set being the normal rigid type, the other being of the swing axle pattern. This car did very little work after about 1930, although it figured in the annual stock returns until and including 1935. It is suspected that it slowly disintegrated in the depot, probably being cannibalised for spares for the other cars.

Of the bogie cars, only one, No. 36, had a thorough rebuilding, being given a new body which was virtually an elongated version of those fitted to the rebuilt small cars, having five windows. The ½-turn stairs were replaced by ¼-turn direct ones, again like the four-wheeled cars, and route light " cupboards " were fitted. Nos. 31 to 35 received normal maintenance only, although this amounted to near rebuilding at times, but in their later years they were remarkably " bowed down " at the ends. All six eight-wheeled cars received new longitudinal interior seating in place of their former transverse reversible seats.

A development which, had it been pursued further, would have been a great improvement, was the fitting, in 1927, of Metropolitan Vickers type 102 DR, 50 h.p. motors to bogie cars Nos. 31 and 32, together with controllers by the same makers. Magnetic track brakes were included in the alterations and the resulting cars were very fast, soon earning a reputation for themselves in Reading, although not wholly a good

Photo courtesy W. A. Camwell.

Rebuilt bogie car No. 36. Note direct stairs and compare with illustration on page 38: This view shows car awaiting scrapping on the Caversham Road siding, in 1937.

one. The trouble was with the track brakes, which very few motormen seemed to like or to master. These brakes were of course operated by the brake notches on the controllers, as were the ordinary rheostatic emergency brakes on the rest of the cars. The fact seemed firmly fixed in the drivers' minds that any notches past the " off " position were for emergency only, and they still continued to wind on their hand brakes for service stops when driving Nos. 31 or 32. With their higher speed, these two cars naturally took greater effort to stop, and they suffered the serious defect of wheel locking and consequent " flats " in the tyres when drivers persisted in using the hand brake. Furthermore, their higher speed was wasted, as no general speed up of services could be made with only two cars so fitted; indeed, it was the greatest dread of many drivers to find themselves the car in front of, or behind 31 or 32, and to have to try and maintain correct headway. The only time when these cars could be used to advantage was in the early morning with only a few cars running on the workmen's service. On one such occasion, the author's father ran from the Barracks to Cemetery Junction in 11 minutes with No. 31, a journey normally taking 18-20 minutes. On another occasion with the same car and a full standing load, he used the track brakes and pulled up so suddenly that the passenger standing nearest the door fell against it, smashing the glass, fortunately without injury.

The general manager's report for the financial year 1929-30 gives a picture of the state of affairs obtaining at the close of the period covered by this chapter. He said, " . . . the results obtained by the operation of the tramcar services during the past year are to be considered very satisfactory, having regard to present-day conditions of road transport services. In spite of additions to the rolling stock of the undertaking by means of motor omnibuses, it is gratifying to note that there is still an increase in the number of tramcar passengers carried in the year under review. It may seem strange, but nevertheless true, that the tramcar service operated on the main line today is heavier than it ever has been in the history of the undertaking. The number of passengers being carried along the main line, particularly from the Oxford Road terminus to the town centre, has increased to such an extent that during the early hours of the morning a service operates from Oxford Road terminus practically every 2 minutes for a considerable period." He continued, " The condition of the tramcar rolling stock is very satisfactory and every care is exercised to see that the cars which have been rebuilt are maintained in a good condition."

Tramcar passengers for the year, the last complete one in which the entire tramway system was in operation, totalled 12,225,100, an increase of 177,052 on the previous year. Traffic receipts amounted to £76,226 representing 19.33 pence per car mile, while the number of passengers carried equalled 151 journeys per head of the population. The report continues, " . . . the fact that we have carried over twelve million passengers during the past year still proves the usefulness of the tramcar vehicle, when comparing the numbers carried by a similar number of omnibuses. Each day we have 23 tramcars in service (average) operating over 7 miles of streets On the other hand, we have 20 omnibuses in daily use over practically 25 route miles and carrying in the course of a year $4\frac{3}{4}$ million passengers. This comparison will perhaps convey some idea as to the number of omnibuses which would be required to perform the duty of conveying such a large number of passengers as is carried at the present time by the tramcars, and will perhaps help you (the Committee) to visualise the conditions of street traffic congestion, should buses at any future time be substituted for tramcars."

CHAPTER VII.

THE DECLINING YEARS—1930 ONWARDS.

The years 1928 and 1929 can be regarded as the zenith of tramway operation in Reading. The cars had been reconditioned, tracks relaid and the undertaking generally was in better shape than it had been for many years. The motor omnibus side of the undertaking was growing, but so far it had served as a feeder to the tramways rather than a competitor. There was little to choose between tram and bus as regards comfort, for buses were still open-topped and solid tyres had only just disappeared. The town was still growing and in June, 1929, the general manager was instructed to submit a report upon the question of extending the Oxford Road tramway from the present terminus to Tilehurst Station, a distance of about a mile and a quarter. At the same time he was also asked to report upon the possibility of substituting trackless trolley vehicles for tramway cars.

Oxford Road west of the tram terminus had recently been widened and was now provided with grass verges which would have been ideal for the construction of reserved tracks. In August, 1929, however, Reading placed in service its first top covered motor bus, a Leyland " Titan " low-bridge model, and to this can be traced the first signs of decay of the tramways. The report on the Oxford Road extension was not laid before the Tramways Committee until May, 1930, but it was obvious that a system tied to open-topped cars by reason of the low bridges, could not hope to compete with the new omnibuses. The result was a resolution, " .... that having regard to the general manager's report, no action be taken at the present time with a view to the extension of the Oxford Road tram service."

The Bath Road tram route had always been acknowledged as a " white elephant " and was always the first route to suffer suspension at times of crisis, such as coal strikes. Being a short route, passengers having missed a car, could get to town more quickly by walking than waiting 15 or 20 minutes for the next car. Furthermore, recent motor bus extensions over and beyond the tram tracks to rapidly developing suburbs rendered the tram service redundant and it was not surprising, therefore that the full Council at their meeting on 1st October, 1929, adopted a resolution to consider the possibility of abolishing the Bath Road route. The result was that in December, 1929, it was decided to abandon this route on the 31st March following, the date chosen presumably being for the convenience of the accountants. It was suggested that the London Road section should be abandoned at the same time as the Bath Road line, but the general manager advised against this and the following service was operated from 1st April, 1930 in lieu of the London Road to Bath Road cars : —

London Road—Broad Street ...	...	7.00 a.m.-12 noon	(15 mins.)
London Road—Oxford Road	...	12 noon - 8.00 p.m.	(10 mins.)
London Road—Broad Street ...	...	8.00 p.m.-10.30 p.m.	(15 mins.)
London Road—Broad Street ...	...	(Sundays from 2.00 p.m.)	

Several minor, but interesting matters came before the Tramways Committee at this time, one being the application by the Cigarette Automatic Supply Company for permission to install cigarette machines on the cars. Neither this, nor a proposal to fit seats on the platforms for the drivers and conductors was adopted, however. The Oxford Road terminus improvement plan was raised once more, but suffered the same fate as previously, while the old hardy annual, transfer tickets reared its head with no more success than hitherto.

In February, 1930, Mr. Calder's chief assistant, Mr. C. H. Stafford, resigned his position, later becoming well known as the manager of Leicester City Tramways. The new chief assistant at Reading was Mr. J. F. Fardell.

The financial year ended 31st March, 1931, produced a net profit of only £683, in spite of a record revenue for the combined tram and bus undertaking of £129,378. This, as the general manager pointed out in his report, indicated that the ratepayers were getting their transport for practically cost price. The primary reason for the small profit was the fact that several new bus services were being operated at a considerable loss, but were necessary as the Road Traffic Act, 1930, had just come into force and it was feared that if the Corporation did not provide the service, road service licences would be granted to other operators and the Corporation would lose a monopoly of traffic within its boundaries. The following figures give a comparison between the trams and motor buses at this date.

Photo Courtesy W. A. Camwell.

Oxford Road terminus as altered for kerbside loading in 1932. This view, taken in 1939, shows Car No. 16 using trolleybus overheads, then recently erected in readiness for changeover.

				Trams	Buses
Number of vehicles	...	...	...	36	31
Routes	...	...	...	3	7
Mileage	...	...	...	7½	30
Outer termini		...	...	6	11
Passengers, 1930-31	...	...		11,721,816	6,195,277

Commencing with the school summer holidays of 1931, a new Juvenile's Holiday Ticket was introduced, at 1d. return any distance. These tickets were issued on trams only and were available on any day, Sundays included, during school holidays (with the exception of August Bank Holiday Monday). A total of 76,603 of these tickets was issued during the month of August, 1931.

The town of Reading, situated at it is at the confluence of the Rivers Thames and Kennet has quite a number of bridges spanning these waterways, particularly the latter. It is perhaps not realised by many Reading people, that the part of King's Road between Crown Bridge and Factory Bridge is actually on an island. Most of the bridges were fairly old structures, and a programme of rebuilding had been prepared, commencing in 1931 with the above-mentioned Crown Bridge, on the main line tramway route. The first step was to lay temporary cross-overs on each side of the bridge to permit single line working on the eastbound track, as the Reading Gas Company's mains lay directly beneath the inner rail of the westbound track and were thus not accessible without interrupting the car service. The bridge, which ran east-west was then divided into three sections, i.e., the northern pavement, the central section carrying the carriageway and the southernmost section with its pavement. The two pavement sections were demolished while the centre section remained in use, following which, new and wider pavement sections were constructed and equipped with temporary tram tracks. When ready the trams (and other traffic) were diverted over the temporary tracks while the centre section was dealt with and the new permanent tram tracks laid thereon. When this stage was completed trams were diverted on to the new track and the temporary tracks removed. These latter tracks had been constructed from rails removed from the abandoned Bath Road line, which necessitated the reinstatement of the surface of that road which, together with the Crown Bridge work, entailed the tramways department in an expenditure of some £3,860, none of which was recoverable as the Ministry of Transport would not grant any financial assistance for work carried out for tramway purposes. Incidentally, all the Crown Bridge scheme had been carried out without once interrupting tramway traffic.

About September, 1931, the Reading Stadium, a greyhound racing track, was opened on a site just west of the Oxford Road tram terminus. The question of alterations to the track layout at this point, several times shelved in the past now arose with considerable urgency. Mr. Calder reported that he had " personally witnessed the chaotic conditions which now obtained in connection with the tramcar and other traffic at this point at the conclusion of meetings." In consultation with the Chief Constable, the Tramways manager prepared a plan which was laid before the Tramways Committee on 19th November, 1931. This proposed to extend the existing double line terminus by bringing the two tracks together to a single line kerbside loading point on the north side of Oxford Road about 150 yards further west. In due course this was carried out at a cost of about £650, under powers contained in the Corporation's 1914 Act, but even then the department's troubles were not at an end. The cars now pulled up very conveniently and safely alongside the footpath, but unfortunately this took place right outside a house, the front room of which was used as a surgery by a local doctor. Passengers sitting on the top decks of cars could now look down on proceedings in the consulting room, to which quite naturally both doctor and patients objected! This difficulty was overcome by painting a white line across the tram track and instructing drivers to bring their cars to a stand clear of the line. Incidentally, the manner in which this was done always struck the writer as rather curious. Instead of painting the line in such a position that the leading end of an incoming car stopped by it, drivers were required to run right over the line and bring the rear ends of their cars to rest clear of the mark. This called for judgment, extra distance being required of course for a bogie car.

About the time of the Oxford Road alterations, the local representative of the Automobile Association approached the tramways department on the matter of altering the London Road terminus. The layout here was double line with a trailing cross-over and owing to the position of the tracks it was practically impossible for other eastbound vehicles to pass on the near side of a tramcar standing at the terminus. They were thus forced on to the off side of the tram into the face of traffic coming the other way. It was agreed to alter the layout to a single line stub in the centre of the road, which permitted vehicles in both directions to pass comfortably. The work was carried out at a cost of £275 in 1932.

In March, 1932, the manager reported that the state of the tram tracks on the Erleigh Road route was such that it would soon be advisable to withdraw the tramcar service and substitute motor buses. The tram service consisted of a car every 7½ minutes to Caversham and Whitley alternately, and in place of this it was proposed to provide a ten minute omnibus service by re-routing the existing " Roebuck " to " Three Tuns " 20 minute service and dovetailing it with an extension of the Tilehurst-Railway Stations route also operating every 20 minutes. The question of fares was a knotty one, as there were no 1½d. fares on the motor buses at that time, and the 1½d. tram fare from Erleigh Road to Duke Street would thus become 2d. This was the subject of much discussion both in the Tramways Committee and the whole Council, the matter being referred back and forth several times in the three months preceeding abandonment. The introduction of a 1½d. bus fare would create a precedent and was not advisable economically as the manager stated that of the eight omnibus services now running the only one paying its way was the Tilehurst service, and the omnibus side of the undertaking had been running at a loss since 1928. In view of this the 1½d. bus fare was not introduced. The trams ceased running to Erleigh Road on 7th August, 1932, following which the Caversham-Whitley section was operated as a straight route with a 7½-minute service.

From the date of abandonment of the Erleigh Road tramway, the Tilehurst and " Roebuck " motor bus services commenced running over the same road as the trams all the way from Broad Street to the Oxford Road terminus, providing between them a 10-minute bus service in competition with the trams, with, however, a protective fare. The result was naturally a drop in tramcar receipts and with a view to economy a car was withdrawn from the Oxford Road-Wokingham Road service after 7.0 p.m., leaving ten cars to provide a 5 minute service and the London Road service was modified as under :—

London Road—Broad Street	...	...	7.00 a.m.-12 noon (2 cars).
London Road—Barracks	...	...	12 noon - 7.00 p.m. (3 cars).
London Road—Broad Street	...	...	7.00 p.m.-10.30 p.m. (2 cars).

This provided a 15-minute service on the London Road branch all day. Sundays two cars worked London Road-Broad Street as before. The cutting back of the London Road cars to the Barracks eased the position on the single-track section between that point and Oxford Road terminus, where they had often " got in the way " of main line cars. As " Barracks " was not on the destination blinds the " Wantage Road " indication was used for about a year, after which many cars were equipped with entirely new blinds embodying several alterations. The abandoned routes were naturally omitted, and the following indications provided : —

Wokingham Road.
Oxford Road.
London Road.
Wantage Road.
Barracks   (new indication).
Broad Street.
Caversham *Road* (previously Caversham).
Whitley *Street* (previously Whitley).
Depot   (previously Car sheds).
Special.
Football Special (new indication).

Mention should be made of the reconstruction during 1932 of the office accommodation at Mill Lane Depot. The single-storey traffic office block was completely rebuilt and another storey added to accommodate the general offices which had previously been adjacent to the power station.

A change in the style of painting the cars took place in May, 1933, when No. 15 appeared with the rocker panels plain cream, lined black and red and no fleet name. The large coat of arms on the waist panels was replaced by a smaller version surrounded by a garter on which were the words " Reading Corporation Tramways and Motors." In December following the Tramways Committee was renamed the Transport Committee and the

Photo Courtesy W. A. Camwell.

Car No. 8 with Motorman Chaplin at Oxford Road, showing Coat of Arms with garter.

General Manager and Engineer was restyled Transport Manager and Engineer. Subsequently the wording on the garter surrounding the coat of arms was altered to Reading Corporation Transport. At yet a later date this design was superseded by the arms without the garter, but with a riband bearing the words "County Borough of Reading, Transport Department," this being the final form carried by the tramcars.

Repainting of rolling stock was always done in numerical order from 1 to 36, after which No. 1 revisited the paint shop again. Cars ran about two years between repaints. It is interesting to note also, that the gold lining out was retained on the cars until the end, although it had long given way to painted lining on the motor buses. In his report for the year 1933-34, however, the Transport Manager stated that the tramcar rolling stock was being maintained in a sound condition, care being exercised to carry out the usual repair work with economy having regard to the fact that a number of tramcars would be discarded within a reasonable period.

In May, 1934, the manager was authorised to hire for an experimental period of three months, nine "T.I.M." ticket machines, following which 120 machines of this type were purchased and have remained the standard ticket system of the department ever since.

The next of the town's numerous bridges to be rebuilt was the renowned Factory Bridge, so called because of its proximity to "The Factory." To Reading people, even today when many new industries have come to the town, there is only one "Factory," that of Huntley and Palmer,

Photo Courtesy W. A. Camwell.
**Car No. 28 at Oxford Road terminus showing final style of livery.
Motorman T. Clark.**

Ltd., the well-known biscuit manufacturers. The steep curved approach to this bridge on the western side was mentioned several times in the chapters dealing with the horse tramways, and plans for the new structure included the easing of the curvature and gradient, demolition of all property on the south side of Kings Road between Watlington Street and the bridge and the laying out of private gardens for the use of Huntley and Palmers' employees on the site. In July, 1934, the chairman and vice-chairman of the Transport Committee were appointed to discuss with the Highways Committee the question of passenger transport services during the period of the reconstruction work. It was decided that a single tram track should be laid on the temporary bridge which was to be erected on the east side of the old bridge, but as this temporary structure was intended to carry eastbound traffic only, it would not be possible to run westbound tramcars over it and the service would therefore have to be cut and shuttle services operated to and from the bridge on either side, passengers crossing the bridge on foot. Ordinary westbound vehicular traffic was to be diverted along Queen's Road and Duke Street. Tramcars on the section remote from the depot would only use the temporary bridge night and morning for the purpose of running to and from depot.

It was intended that the main line tramway route would be abandoned by the time the new bridge was completed and the Council had resolved not to lay a tram track on the new structure. Under these arrangements then, work began on the site on 2nd July, 1935, and the shuttle tram services were introduced. The ordinary 5-minute service was maintained between Oxford Road and the bridge connecting with a similar service on the other side to Wokingham Road, and with a 10-minute service to London Road, which terminus benefitted thereby as it normally only had a 15-minute service. On Sundays the London Road cars connected with a 20-minute service to Caversham. As may be imagined, this method of operation was far from popular with the public, especially in wet weather, and certainly did not enhance the public opinion regarding trams in general. Although a tramway regulator was stationed at the bridge to see that the cars connected with each other, delays were inevitable and in order to ease the situation slightly, special motor buses were put on during peak hours between Broad Street and Wokingham Road at a flat fare of 2d., with a 10-minute frequency.

Public dissatisfaction with these arrangements, however, caused the matter to be re-examined, with the result that on 24th October, 1935, through running with the trams was restored. To achieve this it was necessary to hold up eastbound traffic at the temporary bridge every time a westbound tramcar required to cross, for which purpose manually operated signal lights were installed worked by a police constable in conjunction with a traffic regulator of the tramways. Arrangements had also to be made for the temporary cutting off of the current on the section across the bridge when the jib of the crane working there was required to come close to the tramway overhead wires. The traffic regulator was provided with a key to the special feeder pillar box for this purpose. One result of the restoration of through running was the withdrawal of the bogie cars as they were too long to negotiate the temporary bridge with its limited clearances on the curves. They were stored on a special siding laid in a yard in Caversham Road on the site of the present Central Fire Station and were thereafter only brought out on Saturdays for football specials between Broad Street and Wantage Road, and other similar events.

It became apparent by January, 1936, that the resolution not to lay tram-

**Car No. 9 at London Road terminus in 1938. Motorman Jordan and
Conductor Stone with T.I.M. ticket system.**

way tracks on the new bridge would have to be modified, as it would not
be possible to abandon the trams by the time the new bridge was opened.
It was eventually decided to lay a single track only on the bridge. This was
done and was ready for connecting up to the tracks on either side by 8th
September, 1936. On this date through tram services were again cut, but
on this occasion cars on the far side of the bridge were unable to run to
and from depot as the temporary bridge was being dismantled, so between
the above date and 3rd October, 1936, cars Nos. 3, 14, 17, 19, 24, 26 and
27 were isolated, being parked at the termini at night. When through running was resumed the single line section on the bridge was controlled by
automatic tramway signal lights, and westbound tramcars ran on the right
hand (wrong) side of the " keep left " bollards placed in the centre of the
carriageway. A large warning board was provided for eastbound traffic—
" Motorists, beware approaching tram." On completion the bridge became
known as King's Bridge.

The wrong side running mentioned in the previous paragraph became
quite a habit with the Reading tramways, as it occurred in St. Mary's Butts
after the widening of that thoroughfare in 1932. Here similarly, cars ran
on the righthand side of " keep left " signs, but as the roadway was very
wide at this point there was not so much inconvenience to traffic in the
opposite direction. In the narrow part of Southampton Street above Pell
Street on the Whitley route, a facing cross-over was provided to enable
southbound cars to use the opposite track when their own track was blocked
by lorries parked outside adjacent business premises. In this case a second

**View at Factory Bridge after rebuilding. Car No. 17 is just entering
the single track section. Note warning sign.**

cross-over enabled them to regain their correct track after running about
120 yards on the wrong side of the road. This wrong side running was
covered by Section 14 of the 1899 Reading Tramways Order. Yet another
case of trams keeping to the right, occurred with depot-bound cars in London Street, where, as there was only a depot connection to the inward line
of the Erleigh Road route, cars coming off service were on the wrong side
of the road from the end of the single track over High Bridge to the
corner of Mill Lane.

An extension of the availability of workmen's tickets was made in February, 1936, when they became valid for return at any time on Saturdays
instead of until 1.30 p.m. only.

A Tramways (Future Policy) Sub-committee had been in existence since
December, 1931, charged with consideration of what type of vehicle should
be operated if and when the tramways were abandoned. After numerous
meetings and visits to other towns operating trolley vehicles, it was decided
to recommend that the remaining tramways should be converted to trolleybus operation, and that a Provisional Order be applied for to authorise the
use of these vehicles on the Caversham-Whitley route. About the same time,
however, the Corporation were taking steps to promote a Bill in Parliament
in connection with the purchase of the Reading Electric Supply Company,
and the Parliamentary Agents suggested that it would be more advantageous
to include therein clauses for trolleybus powers in respect of all tram routes
than to proceed with the Provisional Order. This was accordingly done
and the Bill became the Reading Corporation Act, 1935.

The work of converting the Caversham-Whitley tramway began about
May, 1936, and tramcar operation ceased on 15th July, 1936. Motor buses

provided the service for a couple of days, to enable the contractors, Clough, Smith and Co., Ltd., of Westminster, to remove the remains of the tramway overhead, and the trolleybuses commenced running on 18th July, 1936, No. 1 being driven by the Mayor, Councillor W. H. Bale, at the inaugural ceremony. Training of trolleybus drivers was carried out on a specially erected length of overhead in Erleigh Road, utilising the old tramway standards, and at certain times of the day, members of the public were given free rides on this section to enable them to sample the new vehicles. For operating the new service six trolleybuses were obtained, five new ones and a secondhand demonstration bus, which latter was equipped with trolley and skate gear enabling it to be run over ordinary tramways. These vehicles were by different makers for the purpose of comparison, with a view to selecting a standard type for future use, as under :—

No. 1	Sunbeam (secondhand).	No. 4	Leyland.
2	A.E.C.	5	Ramsome.
3	Guy.	6	Sunbeam.

On the final abandonment of the trams in 1939, these buses were renumbered 101-106. All of them have now been withdrawn from service.

Just prior to the opening of the first trolleybus route. Work had begun on the demolition of the car sheds preparatory to the erection of a new garage for the fleet of trolleybuses which would be required to operate the main line when trams were finally withdrawn. To accommodate the tramcars meanwhile, temporary tracks were laid down in the small bus garage on the east side of the power station, the buses so displaced being housed in various buildings in the town temporarily rented for the purpose.

The power station plant which had been in continuous use since the opening of the electric tramways was now 33 years old and in need of replacement. It was decided to discontinue generating current at Mill Lane and to take an E.H.T supply of alternating current from the Corporation

Photo Courtesy H. B. Priestley.

Photograph shows cars in temporary accommodation provided by laying tracks in omnibus garage. This arrangement lasted from 1936 until final abandonment in 1939.

Electricity Department, transforming and rectifying it to the required D.C. traction voltage. The necessary equipment was obtained from the Hewettic Electric Co., Ltd., of Walton on-Thames, the changeover being accomplished without a hitch on 31st October, 1936. The old steam-driven generators were sold as scrap and the boiler house converted into repair shops.

After the abandonment of the Caversham route, the London Road Sunday service during the summer was cut back to London Road and Broad Street. In carrying out the conversion of the Caversham-Whitley tramway, no provision was made in the first instance of negative feeder cables, the abandoned tram rails being used to carry return current. Following representations from the Board of Trade, however, negative feeders were laid in.

With the exception of No. 10 mentioned previously, no cars had yet been withdrawn from service, but the six bogie cars were now isolated in their siding in Caversham Road. They had last been used on 11th January, 1936, when all six were in operation as football specials. Since their semi-retirement incidentally they had had all their brasswork, including hand-rails, controllers and brake handles, and dash lamp rims painted black, giving them a most sombre appearance. Nos. 31 and 32 were broken up in May, 1937, followed by the remainder in November the same year.

Of the single truck cars Nos. 4 and 5 were taken out of traffic in August, 1936, and dumped intact in the depot yard, being joined by No. 28 in October and No. 12 in November, 1936. On Christmas eve, No. 16 was involved in a rather bad collision with Corporation bus No. 2 (Leyland) in Oxford Road, receiving severe damage as a result of which this car also joined the collection in the yard. All these cars, however, were not yet destined for scrapping, as in January, 1937, No. 5 exchanged trucks with No. 30 and reappeared painted in a flat unvarnished maroon with cream rocker panels but completely devoid of any lining out. A week later No. 18

Car No. 5 as decorated for the Coronation of T.M. King George VI and Queen Elizabeth in 1937.

83

was turned out in a similar state. No. 4 was not so fortunate and was broken up, followed by No. 12 a month later. Some cannibalisation took place, among other items, No. 12's controllers were put into No. 11 to replace a very old pair. Surprisingly in March, 1937, No. 28 reappeared completely reconditioned and repainted in full livery, the body having been braced by metal bands bolted to the body corner pillars and joined across the top deck floor. Shortly afterwards Nos. 21 and 29 received similar bracing and the damaged No. 16 reappeared fully restored and repainted.

To celebrate the Coronation of T.M. George VI and Queen Elizabeth in May, 1937, the resurrected No. 5 was decorated and illuminated by hundreds of bulbs and ran thus for a week, being broken up immediately afterwards. It should be mentioned here that No. 6 had been similarly decorated for the Silver Jubilee of King George V and Queen Mary in 1935. No. 18 lingered for a further two months and finally disappeared in July, 1937.

There were now twenty-five cars left in service, Nos. 1-3/6-9/11/13-17/19-30. Repainting continued in numerical order until 18th August, 1938, when No. 11 was turned out, being the last car to receive such treatment. On 29th November, 1938, No. 26 was involved in a collision with a Corporation Electricity Department lorry during a thick fog, suffering severe damage which it was not deemed worth while repairing, so the stock was reduced to 24 cars all of which remained in use until final abandonment. About this time the six trolleybuses had their wheeled trolley heads replaced by the carbon insert skid type, the wheeled heads being fitted to 12 of the trams. The wheels of these heads were larger and had a deeper groove than the standard tramcar type.

In June, 1938, the Great Western Railway Company undertook the rebuilding of their bridge in Oxford Road, the old brick arch being replaced by a plate girder structure of almost twice the span, to allow for road widening. This work necessitated the tram service being cut and temporary cross-overs were inserted on each side of the bridge to enable cars to turn. From 18th-26th June, 1938, Oxford Road was closed to all traffic at this point, and a shuttle service of trams operated on either side of the obstruction. Cars were able to get to and from depot, however, by being towed under the bridge.

Although the 1935 Act contained powers to convert all the existing tramways to trolley vehicle routes, it was decided that when this was done, certain motor bus routes which were in effect extensions of the tram routes, should be converted too. To this end a Provisional Order had been obtained in 1936, to include among others the following sections of motor bus routes.

(a) From Wokingham Road tram terminus to Earley (Three Tuns).

(b) From Oxford Road tram terminus to Tilehurst (Plough) motor bus terminus together with an extension to the Bear Inn.

(c) A turning circle at the junction of Norcot Road and Oxford Road.

Work on the erection of the overhead on these routes began in the closing months of 1938, by Messrs. Clough Smith and Company, the same contractors as employed for the Caversham-Whitley conversion, and who incidentally included in their equipment for this " modernisation " a horse tower wagon ! As soon as the section west of Oxford Road tram terminus was completed it was brought into use for the purpose of training drivers after their initial tuition on the Erleigh Road section. The Ministry of Transport driving tests were conducted on the Tilehurst section in preference to

Oxford Road railway bridge in 1938 just prior to replacement by a girder bridge. Note "Keep your seats" warning to tram passengers.

Photo H. E. Jordan.

Car No. 29 in Oxford Road on Football Special service. Note overhead ready for trolleybuses.

Erleigh Road, as the former embodied almost all possible situations, viz., right- and left-hand turns, turning circles, a " Y " reverser and hills.

On the 1st May, 1939, notices appeared on the tramcars that, " Circumstances permitting the new main line trolleybus route will be opened for the conveyance of passengers on Sunday, 21st May, 1939. A further announcement will be made later." This announcement duly appeared stating : —

> " Tramcars will not run again after Saturday night, 20th May, 1939. The last tram will leave Broad Street for Depot at 11.30 o'clock on that night."

At 10.30 p.m. on " the night," the usual gathering of civic dignitaries assembled and boarded two of the new trolleybuses and proceeded to Oxford Road terminus, where they awaited the arrival of the last car. This was

No. 13, which was completely devoid of any special decoration having been in normal service all day. The car was driven by the oldest motorman, Mr. W. E. Dew with the oldest conductor, Mr. H. Burkett, and on arrival at the terminus was boarded by the official party which included the Mayor, Councillor W. E. McIlroy, the chairman of the Transport Committee, Councillor Bennet Palmer, the Transport manager, Mr. Calder, and other members and officials of the Council. Also present was Mr. G. F. Craven, the former Tramways manager who had travelled specially from Halifax for the occasion. All passengers on the car were issued with special souvenir tickets marked " Reading Corporation Transport—Ticket issued on last tram from Pond House to Journey's End 20th May, 1939. A.D. 1903-1939, For Conditions see back." On the reverse side was one word, " NIL."

Photo Courtesy Berkshire Chronicle.

The last tram. No. 13 leaving Oxford Road terminus 20th May, 1939.

The Mayor and chairman took turns in driving the car back to Depot amid cheering crowds. On reaching Broad Street a band from a nearby dance hall provided an unofficial accompaniment by walking in front of the car all the way to Mill Lane playing such tunes as " Old Faithful " and " Auld Lang Syne." Depot was reached just before midnight.

Last cars from the other termini were, No. 14, at 11.15 p.m. from Wokingham Road, with motorman F. Clark and conductor Cullingham, and from London Road, No. 21 at 10.45 p.m. with motorman H. E. Jordan, senr. (assisted by a near relative and friends) with conductor W. May.

The official ceremony at Mill Lane Depot closed with refreshments and speeches, in the course of which the chairman was reported in several journals as saying that the trams in their 36 years life ran some $12\frac{1}{2}$ million miles, carried 155 million passengers and took over two million pounds in traffic receipts. With all respect to the chairman and his reporters, the present writer is unable to reconcile these figures with official reports, with the exception of cash receipts. Car mileage was nearer 30 million and passengers carried in the neighbourhood of 350 million if the general manager's annual statements to his committee are to be relied on. In any case these astronomical figures convey very little to the average reader except the fact that Reading's trams served the town well.

CHAPTER VIII.

AFTER ABANDONMENT.

To all intents and purposes the previous chapter brings to an end the story of Reading's tramways, but for the sake of completeness the following details of subsequent developments are included. The twenty-four tramcars in use at the end were sold for £456, or £19 each. They were bought by Grahamsleys, Ltd., of South Gosforth, Newcastle, and with the exception of a few bodies sold locally, this firm broke the cars up where they stood in the depot. Of those sold, No. 14 became a garden shed at Southend Post Office, between Bradfield and Bucklebury, Berks, while No. 24 was used as an office at a gravel pit at Sonning, near Reading. Two more were converted into sheds on some allotments in School Lane, Caversham, where ironically, they served as a reminder of the two fruitless schemes to run trams in that district. Another car body stood in a garden in May's Lane, Earley, Reading, until it was broken up in 1955. When used in this way old bus and tram bodies tend to become eyesores, but quite the neatest use was made of two of the vestibuled cars at Purley Park Estate, near Reading where the vestibule ends were used to form bay windows of a bungalow.

The trolleybus services introduced on the 21st May, 1939, in place of the trams were as follows : —

Route A   Three Tuns (Wokingham Road)—Tilehurst (Bear Inn).
     B   Three Tuns—Norcot Junction.
     D   London Road—Norcot Junction.
     (Route C was the Caversham-Whitley service.)

Route B (roughly the equivalent of the Wokingham Road-Oxford Road tram service) was actually a short working of the " A," the two services combining to provide a basic frequency of 5 minutes between Three Tuns and Norcot Junction and a 10/20-minute service beyond Norcot on the Tilehurst route. Route D ran every 15 minutes and extras were provided at peak hours. Services were worked by 25 new A.E.C.-E.E.C. 56-seat double-deck vehicles, Nos. 107-131, all of which are still in existence at the present time (October, 1956).

Less than four months after the abandonment of the tramways the country was again involved in war and one is tempted to wonder if the trams would have been scrapped so soon could this have been foreseen. Wartime conditions threw a terrific burden on the new vehicles and Reading people soon grew accustomed to conductors' cries of " Full up," a thing unknown in tram days. A rather amusing sidelight on the relative capacities of trams and buses was unintentionally provided by a form issued to conductors. In tram days, this form was headed " Overload Report " and provided spaces for reporting " Number of passengers standing " and " Reason (if any) for overloading." The equivalent bus form was styled a " Full-up Report " and instead of the above mentioned sections, there were spaces for " Passengers left behind at the following places " and " Number left." In fairness to the trolleybuses, it should be stated that on their introduction, fare stages were lengthened, tantamount to a reduction of fares.

Owing to the war, some of the trolleybus routes authorised by the Provisional Order of 1936 were not proceeded with, and the powers lapsed in 1941, the Ministry of War Transport stating that they were unable to entertain any application for renewal of same. In 1943, however, permission was granted under Defence Regulations 54B and 56 for the construction of a trolleybus route along Oxford Road from Norcot Junction to Kentwood, near Tilehurst railway station, a distance of 1,420 yards, thus fulfilling a proposal made many years before the abandonment of the trams. Work on this extension commenced early in 1944 and the route was opened to traffic on 31st July that year. It replaced a motor bus service, saving some 9,500 gallons of diesel fuel per year, this fact contributing largely to the Ministry's favourable consideration of the project. The service was provided by extending buses on route B beyond Norcot Junction.

There was no further trolleybus development during the war, in fact the Caversham-Whitley service was reduced and later completely suspended as motor buses were covering the same roads and serving points beyond the Whitley terminus. After the war, another Provisional Order was obtained in 1946 authorising further extensions which resulted in the Caversham-Whitley route reopening as part of a much longer route from Caversham Bridge to Northumberland Avenue, on which services commenced on 5th June, 1949. On the 7th August following, the short branch to Reading Stations was opened, together with the extension to Whitley Wood, again replacing a motor bus service. Very recently (December, 1955) the Reading Council approved in principle the extension of the Kentwood route to Armour Hill to serve a new housing estate, but so far this project has not got beyond the " talking " stage.

To conclude the account of services, the following summarises those operating at the present time over former tram routes.

Tram route		Present service
Wokingham Road—Oxford Road.	Trolleybus,	Wokingham Road—Norcot—Tilehurst.
London Road branch.	,,	Liverpool Road—Norcot—Kentwood.
Caversham—Whitley.	,,	Caversham Bridge—Northumberland Avenue.
	,,	Stations—Northumberland Avenue.
	,,	Stations—Whitley Wood.
Erleigh Road.	Motor bus,	Erleigh Road—Grovelands.
Bath Road.	,,	Southcote—Donkin Hill.
	,,	Horncastle—Hemdean Road.
	,,	Erleigh Road—Grovelands.

Of the present day termini, only two remain as they were in the time of the trams, Erleigh Road and Caversham (Bridge). Of the others, London Road is now known as Liverpool Road by reason of the fact that trolleybuses leave the main road and traverse side streets in order to turn, the actual terminus stand being in the latter road. At Whitley an ornamental garden forms the centre of a traffic roundabout on the site of the terminus, and although a trolleybus turning circle is still provided there and " Whitley Street " appears on destinaton blinds, no regular services operate to this point which is used for emergency turning only. All other former tram termini are now merely stopping places on the respective routes.

In tram days, complaints were often made that tramcars standing in the middle line in Broad Street constituted a danger and obstruction to traffic. When the rails were lifted and the road resurfaced, a large island refuge was placed in exactly the same spot; so whereas before the only (alleged) obstruction was from the occasional tram standing there, a permanent obstruction now exists, but no one seems to mind in the least !

Comparison of tram fares with those charged today is, of course, pointless, in view of the vastly increased operating costs, but it is of interest to note the following examples : —

Fare from Wokingham Road tram terminus to Oxford Road tram terminus—

in 1903	...	...	2d.
in 1939	...	...	3d.
in 1956	...	...	6d.

Fare from Caversham tram terminus to Whitley tram terminus—

in 1903	...	...	1d.
in 1939	...	...	2d.
in 1956	...	...	4d.

All forms of cheap or concession fares available on the trams have now been abolished. These comprised Discount Tickets, Juvenile's Holiday Returns and Workmen's Returns.

Physical remains of the tramways exist in the form of buried tracks, the following sections being " visible " under a layer of tar at the present time : —

The entire section from Cemetery Junction to Wokingham Road tram terminus.

In Kings Road between Eldon Road and Factory Bridge and again for a short distance on Crown Bridge.

In Duke Street over High Bridge and continuing into London Street, thence into Mill Lane depot.

Most of Caversham Road from Friar Street to the terminus.

In London Road (Erleigh Road route) between London Street corner and Albion Place.

Nearly all the above sections are scheduled for lifting.

On a recent visit to a new housing estate at Tilehurst, the author was intrigued to find among the builders' materials a considerable stack of tram rails. Hardly daring to believe a new tramway was to be laid to serve the estate, enquiries were made which revealed that the rails were being utilised as girders in the construction of the houses. Still more recently a number of short lengths of about 18 in. each were observed in the Mill Lane depot yard stencilled " R.C.T. 56 lb." The exact purpose of these has not been discovered, but it is evident that after 16 years abandonment, the " way " is still pretty " permanent."

The old power station building and boiler house still stand in Mill Lane, although now used as a substation and repair shops respectively. Built into the front wall of the boiler house is a large stone slab bearing the words "Reading Corporation Tramways—Power Station—1903," but today this is boarded up to conceal the inscription, not through any desire to obliterate reference to the tramways, but because during the late war all indications of place names were removed for security reasons.

These then are the last few remaining links with the Reading trams; links which in the course of time will disappear in an age of jet propulsion and atomic power. Future generations will not know the exhilaration of a ride in the fresh air on the open top deck of a tramcar, childhood memories of which, the author must confess, still cause spasms of nostalgia.

APPENDIX "A"

FARE TICKETS.

P<small>LATE</small> I.

Ticket No.	Description.	Colour.

Horse Tramway Tickets.

4451	Tramways Company 1d.	Salmon.
9770	Corporation 1d.	Pale Pink.

Electric Tramway Tickets.

6401	Ordinary 2d. (early style).	White —Red overprint.
7285	Education Exchange.	Yellow —Red overprint.
9846	1½d. Exchange.	Buff —Red overprint.
7267	2d. Exchange.	Salmon—Red overprint.
8616	1d. Parcel.	White with Blue vertical stripe —Red overprint.

P<small>LATE</small> II.

6322	Ordinary 1d.	Red.
3802	Ordinary 1½d.	Blue.
8778	Workman's Return 2d.	Brown.
1181	Workman's Exchange.	Lilac —Red overprint.
5636	Juvenile Holiday Return 1d.	Yellow.
2304	Ordinary 3d.	Green.

APPENDIX "B"

TRAMCAR AXLE BREAKAGES

Further to the reference to broken axles on page 37, this defect persisted throughout the life of the tramways, and an interesting document has come to light (dated 8/3/34) recording all such occurrences in the 21 year period 1913 – 1933. It lists the number of breakages suffered by each individual car from which the following analysis has been extracted.

Car No.	Breakages		Year	Breakages
1	8		1913	16
2	7		1914	19
3	6		1915	17
4	5		1916	10
5	6		1917	8
6	6		1918	6
7	4		1919	9
8	4		1920	7
9	2		1921	10
10	2		1922	8
11	8		1923	7
12	3		1924	4
13	7		1925	4
14	7		1926	2
15	6		1927	5
16	6		1928	7
17	3		1929	5
18	3		1930	9
19	6		1931	2
20	8		1932	7
21	4		1933	5
22	3			
23	7		TOTAL	167
24	6			
25	7			
26	6			
27	5			
28	9			
29	5			
30	3			
Bogie car 31	1	(Driving axle)		
Bogie car 32	2	(Driving axle)		
Bogie cars 33-36	NIL			
Water car 37	2			

TOTAL 167

It is interesting to note that the only cars completely free of trouble were the four bogie cars 33-36, although their sisters 31 and 32 did not escape. Even the little used Water Car 37 suffered two mishaps. There may be some significance in the fact that the worst years were during the period of war time maintenance difficulties and heavy loading.

READING CORPORATION TRANSPORT —

QUESTIONS TO INTENDING MOTORMEN

1   What is the first thing you would do on taking a car out of the Depot?
Answer Try sand gear, gong, see spare fuses, try brake.

2   What is the first thing you would do after bringing a car into the Depot?
Answer Knock out the switches.

3   How would you know the electric brake was in order?
Answer I should try it at the first opportunity.

4   In case you could not stop the car with the hand brake, what might this be due to, in addition to the brakes not being properly set?
Answer The wheels might be locked, especially during foggy weather when the rail is bad.

5   What would you do to prevent this?
Answer Release brake slightly and apply sand, then put the brake on again.

6   When would you use the electric brake?
Answer Only in case of emergency.

7   Is it possible to have the same trouble (wheels skidding) with the electric brake?
Answer Yes.

8   How would this difficulty be obviated?
Answer At all times, whether the rail is in good condition or not, sand must be applied continuously at the same time as the electric brake is applied, and on no account should the motorman wait to see if the car can be stopped without sand, otherwise the accident will happen before the second trial can be made.

9   Is the brake operative with the trolley off the wire??
Answer Yes.

10   How does it operate?
Answer Connection is made by the controller so that the motors acting as generators have to do an amount of work which stops them.

11   How does the current pass from the overhead line back to the Power Station?
Answer Trolley wheel, trolley head, trolley cable (through trolley standard), automatic canopy switch, fuse, controller cables, motors, wheels and rails.

12   How are the motors running when the controller is on first notch?
Answer Motors are running in series.

13   What is the object of the first three notches and Nos. 5 and 6?
Answer To keep down the current supply until motors have properly started.

14   How is the car running on the first four notches?
Answer In series.

15   And on the last three notches?
Answer In parallel.

16   What is meant by "series"?
Answer The current passes through No. 1 motor and then through No. 2 motor before returning via the rail to the Power Station.

17   How does the current pass through the motors in parallel?
Answer The current goes through the controller and there divides. Two distinct circuits are made through the motors.

18   What would you do in case a controller jammed, to stop the car?
Answer Knock out the canopy or automatic switch and thus cut off the juice. ✳

19   What would you do in the case of a broken axle?
Answer Run on the motor at the opposite end to the broken axle.

20   How would you do that?
Answer Cut out the motor which is on the broken axle.

21   Where do you cut out the motor?
Answer At the controller. (New type — arrow to join motors.)

22   How would you cut out No. 1 motor?
Answer (Intending motorman will here cut out the motor).

23   Cut out No. 2 motor?
Answer Right hand side. (Both bogies and small cars should be tried).

24   In cases where you get no lights and you cannot move the car, what would you assume is the matter with the car?
Answer The car may be grounded.

25   What remedy would you use to overcome this?
Answer Apply water to the track.

26   The current may be off the line — what would you do in that case?
Answer Put light switches on and wait till the current came on. (The trolley cable may be broken, the trolley wire may be insulated by frost.)

27   What is the use of the leakage indicator?
Answer To show that the trolley standard has become alive.

28   What would you do in this case?
Answer Request passengers to leave the top deck and change over the car as soon as possible.

29   Supposing your car will not move and the lights are on, what may be wrong with the car?
Answer One motor may be wrong — most likely a fuse blown.

30   How would you replace the fuse?
Answer Knock out the automatic or canopy switch and then put in the fuse.

31   Suppose you are going up a hill, say Southampton Street, and you apply the hand brake, the car is stopped and suddenly begins to run backwards, what would you do?
Answer Put on power and go to the top of the hill and report the brakes immediately.

32   In case the car runs backwards so rapidly that your switch blew, what would you do??
Answer Put over the reversing handle and apply electric brake (with old controllers). With new controllers leave handle in forward position.

✳ The use of the colloquial "juice" in reference to the power in question 18 should be noted!

95

APPENDIX "D"

DETAILS OF 24 TRAMCARS FOR DISPOSAL

The Corporation have for disposal 24 double deck, open top, single truck tramcars, seating 48 passengers, mounted on Brill 21E traction trucks.

		Author's Note
18 cars are equipped with	Dick Kerr DK25a Motors and Dick Kerr DB1 form K3b Controllers	A
2 cars are equipped with	Dick Kerr DK6a Motors and DB1 Form K3b controllers	B
2 cars are equipped with	Dick Kerr DK6a Motors and DB1 Form B controllers	C
1 car is equipped with	Dick Kerr DK6a Motors and Metro-Vick OK9b controllers	D
1 car is equipped with	Dick Kerr DK20a Motors and DB1 form K3b controllers	E

23 of the above cars are equipped with Dick Kerr Type FR Platform Resistances and one car is equipped with Dick Kerr type DK Under Car resistances. — F

The motor equipment on all cars has been maintained in good condition.

Fifteen of the above tramcars have vestibuled fronts while the remainder have open fronts. — G

The cars run on 4ft gauge track.

All cars will be handed over to the contractor without trolley booms and trolley heads and without the ropes and jacks used for breakdown purposes, and without the longitudinal lower saloon seats.

It is important that all cars should be dismantled and cleared from the Depot with the utmost possible despatch, and the contractor must state in his tender:—

1. How soon after the placing of the contract and the receipt of instructions to proceed, can he commence to dismantle the cars.

2. The number of weeks required for the completion of the contract.

The cars are housed in the Depot at Mill Lane Reading.

Tenders endorsed "Tender for Tramcars" to be delivered to the Town Clerk, Town Hall, Reading, not later than Tuesday February 21st 1939 and to be enclosed in the envelope provided which must not bear any mark indicating the sender.

Reading Corporation Transport Offices.　　　J. M. CALDER
Mill Lane, READING　　　　　　Transport Manager & Engineer
13th February 1939.

AUTHOR'S NOTES
A　—　Cars 1-3/8/9/13-16/19/21-25/27-29.
B　—　Cars 6 and 17
C　—　Cars 7 and 11
D　—　Car 30
E　—　Car 20
F　—　Car 7 had Under car resistances
G　—　This is an error, there were never more than 13 vestibuled cars
　　　— 1/7/8/9/11/15/16/17/19/20/25/29/30.